HOW MUCH TAX DO YOU REALLY PAY ?

The Fraser Institute

The Fraser Institute is an independent Canadian economic and social research and educational organization. It has as its objective the redirection of public attention to the role of competitive markets in providing for the well-being of Canadians. Where markets work, the Institute's interest lies in trying to discover prospects for improvement. Where markets do not work, its interest lies in finding the reasons. Where competitive markets have been replaced by government control, the interest of the Institute lies in documenting objectively the nature of the improvement or deterioration resulting from government intervention.

The work of the Institute is assisted by an Editorial Advisory Board which includes:

The Fraser Institute is a national, federally-chartered, non-profit organization financed by the sale of its publications and the contributions of its members.

Orders for publications and membership enquiries should be addressed to:

THE FRASER INSTITUTE
626 Bute Street,
Vancouver, British Columbia
Canada V6E 3M1

Telephone (604) 688-0221

HOW MUCH TAX DO YOU REALLY PAY ?

Your real tax guide

Introducing the Canadian Consumer Tax Index

SALLY PIPES

JOHN RAYBOULD

SPENCER STAR

MICHAEL WALKER (Editor)

THE FRASER INSTITUTE

1976

Canadian Cataloguing in Publication Data
Main entry under title:
How much tax do you really pay?
    Includes bibliography.
    ISBN 0-88975-004-1
1. Taxation—Canada—Addresses, essays,
lectures. I. Walker, Michael, 1945-   II.
Pipes, Sally, 1945-   III. Raybould, V.
John, 1939-   IV.   Star, Spencer, 1942-
HJ2451.H69   336.2′00971   C76-016063-5

First published 1976 by the Fraser Institute.
ISBN 0-88975-004-1 (trade paperback)
Manuscripts processed and tapes set by K. Hay at the
Fraser Institute
Tapes processed by CDH Computype Services Ltd.,
Burnaby, B.C.
Cartoons and charts by Alfred Penz and Herb Doerlich,
Vancouver, B.C.
Printed by Web Offset Ltd., Don Mills, Ontario

Contents

Preface   ix
About the Authors   xii
Glossary — Some of the Principal Terms,
Measures and Concepts used in this Guide   xv

PART ONE

INTRODUCTION   3

PART TWO

CALCULATING THE TAX PAYABLE   9

PART THREE

HOW MUCH DO YOU PAY
FOR GOVERNMENT ?   15
    The crucial questions   17
    The average Canadian   18
    How the average Canadian family
    spends its income   19
    How much tax?   21
    Peeling the income onion   22
    How much income?   25
    Hidden income   25
    One last detour   26
    How much purchasing power
    does government take away?   28
    Tax and the average family   29

PART FOUR

INTRODUCING THE CANADIAN
CONSUMER TAX INDEX   37

What the Index shows —
the tax bite compared   39
Did you get your money's worth?   46
The tax dollar make-up   48

PART FIVE

THE RELATIVE BURDEN OF TAXATION   53

The un-average Canadian   54
The Horatio Alger line   59
Afterword   60

PART SIX

YOUR REAL INCOME AND TAX GUIDE

How to use the Income Tables   67
How to use the Tax Tables   79
How to calculate your **REAL** tax rate   97

Bibliography   98

TABLES

1.	1975 Income Table	23
2.	Income of the Average Canadian Family	28
3.	1975 Tax Table	30
4.	Taxes Paid by the Average Canadian Family	32
5.	Tax Rates of the Average Canadian Family Expressed as a Percentage of Income	33
6.	The Canadian Consumer Tax Index, 1961 = 100	37
7.	Income, Taxes and Selected Expenditures of the Average Canadian Family	40
8.	Average Canadian Tax, Income, Price and Selected Expenditure Indices for Selected Years, 1961 = 100	42
9.	Taxes and Selected Expenditures of the Average Canadian Family Expressed as a Percentage of Total Before-Government Income	44
10.	Incomes, Taxes and Tax Rates of High Income, Average Income and Poverty Line Families	55
11.	The Rags-to-Riches Tax Burden	58

12. Taxes Paid by Low Income, Average Income, and High Income Families — 61
13. Share of Income and Taxes by Low Income, Average Income and High Income Families — 62
14. Net Taxes Paid and Their Share of the Total Paid by Low Income, Average Income and High Income Families — 63

Income Tables

15. 1975 Income Table — 68
16. 1972 Income Table — 71
17. 1969 Income Table — 73
18. 1961 Income Table — 75

Tax Tables

19. 1975 Tax Table — 80
20. 1972 Tax Table — 84
21. 1969 Tax Table — 88
22. 1961 Tax Table — 92

CHARTS

1. Introducing the Canadian Consumer Tax Index — 38
2. Taxes and Selected Expenditures of the Average Canadian Family, 1961-1975 — 41
3. How the Canadian Consumer Tax Index (CTI) has Increased Relative to Other Selected Indices, 1961-1975 — 43
4. Taxes and Selected Expenditures of the Average Canadian Family Expressed as a Percentage of Total Before-Government Income — 45
5. Where the Taxpayer's Total Tax Dollar Went in 1961 and 1975 — 49
6. How Much Tax Do Canadians Pay? Comparison of Tax Rates and Total Taxes Paid on Total Before-Government Income — 57

Preface

This "Guide" is a summary of the results of a Fraser Institute project that began in July, 1975. The objective of the project was to find out how much tax, in all forms, Canadians pay to Federal, Provincial and Municipal governments and how the size of this tax bill has changed from 1961 to the present. The study analyzes Canada's tax system in each of three years, 1961, 1969 and 1972. The years 1961 and 1969 were chosen because they have been the focus of major studies in the past. Neither of these major studies attempted to link their findings together over several years. The Fraser Institute study has done this and has incorporated the 1972 data which are the latest data that have been released by Statistics Canada at the time of this writing; however, we have also prepared estimates for 1975.

It will come as no surprise to anybody that we found the system of taxation to be very complicated and that its structure closely resembles that of an onion. The process of cutting through the layers of taxation also provided its share of tearful moments — both because of its difficulty and because of what we found. We are publishing this Guide to taxation in Canada to make the results of our in-depth study accessible to taxpayers who are concerned about the tax explosion in recent years but have neither the time nor the inclination to wade into the forbidding taxation jungle.

The Guide has been written with two distinct purposes in mind. First, to provide a non-technical do-it-yourself manual so that the average Canadian family can calculate how much tax it really pays. Secondly, to give circulation to a new statistic that we call the Canadian Consumer Tax Index. This Index measures how much the tax bill of an average Canadian family has increased since 1961 and by how much it is changing currently. In other words, it measures changes in the price that Canadians pay for government. It is comparable to the Consumer Price Index which measures changes in the price that Canadians pay for all of the things that they buy.

This is the first time that such a Tax Guide has been published and understandably it has certain weaknesses. For example, it does not enable the taxpayer to adjust his or her tax bill according to the province in which he or she lives. Although this means that variations in sales tax rates (Alberta has none) and differences in income tax rates from province to province are not accounted for, the evidence suggests that once the "dust settles" inter-provincial differences are very minor.† Province by province tabulations are planned for future editions of this Guide.

This Guide does not attempt to look at the benefits that Canadians receive from government in return for their taxes. Rather, it looks at the price that is paid for a product — government. It has nothing to say about the quality of the product, how much of it each of us receives or whether we get our money's worth. These questions, essential though they are, must be considered in another study.

As a first, this Guide will attract many comments, hopefully some of them critical. It will be said by some that we have made too much of the information that we have. Enthusiasts will say that we have not done enough. Inevitably, some of the criticisms will be valid and in subsequent years they will be reflected in the structure and content of the Guide.

The technical study that lies behind and supports the work in this Guide was undertaken by Sally Pipes and Spencer Star. Because the objective of this Guide is to slice through the complexities of the tax structure, it would not have made sense to include in the Guide all of the complex

---

†Allan M. Maslove in his study *The Pattern of Taxation in Canada,* Economic Council of Canada, December 1972, analyzes income and taxation patterns for Canada and the provinces for 1969. From this data, Maslove calculated the tax incidence for the regions under study. He states on page 74, "to summarize the overall tax patterns in Canada, the interprovincial differences are rather slight and are certainly not large enough to alter the basic incidence pattern, which is consistent across Canada." Since 1969 more significant interprovincial differences have arisen and these will be reflected in future editions.

manipulations contained in the Star & Pipes study. However, those who have an interest in all the detail may acquire the technical study, at cost, from the Institute.

The design and layout of this Guide reflect to a large extent the unique talents of John Raybould and I am pleased to acknowledge his assistance in its preparation.

Computer programming assistance was provided by Anthony Pipes and Keith Wales. Several earlier major contributions to the literature in the field of taxation are acknowledged in the bibliography. Certain unpublished background data essential to the study were made available to the Institute by Mrs. Gail Oja, Director, Consumer Income and Expenditure Division, Statistics Canada, to whom we extend our thanks.

July 1976   **Michael Walker**

". . . yet how is it these vital facts are virtually unknown in this country today?"

THE AUTHORS

Sally C. Pipes is a Fraser Institute staff economist. Born in British Columbia in 1945, she graduated in Economics from the University of British Columbia in 1967. Prior to joining the Fraser Institute in 1974, Mrs. Pipes held a variety of research positions in both the private and public sectors, including the Policy and Planning Branch, Federal Department of Energy, Mines and Resources, and the British Columbia Council of Forest Industries. Sally is immediate past-president of the Association of Professional Economists of British Columbia and is currently Secretary of the Canadian Association for Business Economics.

Mrs. Pipes co-authored Fraser Institute Technical Report 76-01, *An Analysis of Income and Taxation in Canada, 1961-1972*, on which much of this Guide is based.

V. John Raybould is Publications Advisor of the Fraser Institute. Born in London, England in 1939, he graduated in Honors History in 1961 from University College London and has pursued graduate studies at the University of London and the University of British Columbia. John's wide-ranging experience in economic research includes a stint as Economic Intelligence Officer with the British Mechanical Engineering Federation, Research Director of the Employers' Council of British Columbia and Socio-Economic Studies Administrator, British Columbia Telephone Company. A person widely-known for his versatility, John initiated the semi-annual "Business Trends Survey" now published by the B.C. Employers' Council and has published a number of research studies relating to the B.C. economy. In addition, he has been a guest lecturer in the School of Architecture at the University of British Columbia. A past-president of the Association of Professional Economists of British Columbia, Mr. Raybould has also been Treasurer of the B.C. Division of the Community Planning Association of Canada and a member of the City of Vancouver's Heritage Advisory Board.

Mr. Raybould was production and distribution coordinator of the Fraser Institute's first two books: "Rent Control - A Popular Paradox", (published October, 1975) and "The Illusion of Wage and Price Control", (published April, 1976).

Spencer Star was born in Chicago in 1942, and received a B.S. (1964) from the University of Illinois, and an M.A. (1965) and PhD. (1971) in Economics from the University of California, Berkeley. He was an Instructor of Economics at the University of California, Berkeley from 1968 to 1969. In 1969 he joined the faculty of Southern Methodist University in Dallas, Texas, and in 1973 he moved to the University of British Columbia in Vancouver where he taught economics until 1975. He then formed a consulting firm, Econ Research and Consulting Ltd., in Vancouver to carry out and direct research for governments and private organizations.

Dr. Star has done extensive research on productivity measurement, index numbers, immigration, public utilities and taxation. He has published scholarly articles in *The American Economic Review, Econometrica* and *Canadian Public Policy* and co-authored Fraser Institute Technical Report 76-01, *An Analysis of Income and Taxation in Canada, 1961-1972.*

Michael A. Walker, PhD., is Chief Economist of the Fraser Institute. Born in Newfoundland in 1945, he received his B.A. (Summa) at St. Francis Xavier University and his PhD. in Economics at the University of Western Ontario, 1969. From 1969 to 1973, he worked in various research capacities at the Bank of Canada, Ottawa and when he left in 1973, was Research Officer in charge of the Special Studies and Monetary Policy group in the Department of Banking. Dr. Walker has also taught Economics and Statistics at the University of Western Ontario and Carleton University. Immediately prior to joining the Fraser Institute, Dr. Walker was Econometric Model Consultant to the Federal Department of Finance, Ottawa.

Dr. Walker was Editor of, and a contributor to, the Fraser Institute's two previous books: "Rent Control - A Popular Paradox" and "The Illusion of Wage and Price Control".

Glossary

SOME OF THE PRINCIPAL TERMS, MEASURES AND CONCEPTS USED IN THIS GUIDE.

ABOUT INDICES

Index: a method of measuring the percentage change from a base year of a certain item, such as the price, volume or value of food or the dollar amount of taxes. In order to construct an Index, the price, volume or value of the particular item being indexed in each year is divided by the price, volume or value of that item in the base year; it is then multiplied by 100. An Index has a value of 100 in the base year; in this book the base year chosen is 1961.

Consumer Price Index: measures the percentage change from a base year in the cost of purchasing a constant "basket" of goods and services representing the purchases by a particular population group in a specified time period. The Consumer Price Index or CPI, as it is often called, reflects price movements of some 300 items. The CPI is calculated monthly by Statistics Canada (see below).

Consumer Tax Index: measures the percentage change from a base year in the average Canadian family's tax bill. The Consumer Tax Index or CTI is composed of some 32 Federal, Provincial and Municipal taxes. The CTI is a new Index, calculated by the Fraser Institute and introduced for the first time in this book.

SOME STATISTICAL TERMS

Statistics Canada: is Canada's official statistical agency which is often referred to as "StatCan". Statistics Canada provided much of the published and unpublished data for this Guide. For a detailed listing of these sources, see the Bibliography.

Average Canadian Family: represents a family that had average income in a particular year. The averages were constructed from Statistics Canada's expenditure survey, details of which appear in the Bibliography.

Family Expenditure Survey: refers to the Statistics Canada surveys which show patterns of family expenditure for Canada by selected characteristics such as urban and/or rural area, family type, life cycle, income, age of head, tenure, occupation of head, education of head, country of origin and, if applicable, immigrant arrival year. The tables in these surveys which were integral to this book were those entitled, "Detailed Average Expenditure by Family Income for All Families and Unattached Individuals". From these tables it was possible to look at the spending patterns of the average family in each income class.

Family: refers to a group of persons dependent upon a common or pooled income for their major expenditure items and living in the same dwelling; the term also applies to a financially-independent unattached individual living alone.

Shelter Expenditure: is included as one of the selected expenditure items in this Guide. It refers to expenditures on rented or owned living quarters; on repairs to these quarters; on mortgage interest and on other housing, such as vacation homes, lodging at university or at remote work locations. It also includes expenditures on water and heating fuel.

Security Expenditure: is included as one of the selected expenditure items in this Guide. This category includes personal insurance and annuities, mutual aid society payments, unemployment insurance and retirement or pension funds whether private or government.

INCOME CONCEPTS USED IN THE GUIDE

Cash Income: is the income that a family would report when completing a government survey, such as the Family Expenditure Survey or the Census form. It includes income that one receives regularly, such as salary or wage income (before tax) and payments from government such as family allowances.

Full Cash Income: is cash income plus extra income that is often omitted when a family speaks of its income. Items that are often excluded from cash income include bond or bank interest and dividend income.

Income from Government: is income that a family receives as payment **from** the government, whereas taxes are payments **to** the government. Therefore, income from government can be considered a "negative tax", often referred to as **transfer payments.** It includes such items as family allowance payments, old age security payments, veterans' grants, etc.

Hidden Income: is income that a family receives but probably does not consider to be part of its income. Hidden income is largely made up of employer contributions to pension plans, medical premiums and insurance plans. Another example is imputed non-farm rent. (For a more complete discussion of imputed non-farm rent see the Fraser Institute publication "Rent Control - A Popular Paradox", p. 33).

Hidden Purchasing Power Loss: the prices of articles that the family buys are higher by the amount of hidden taxes which are paid to government by an intermediary and not at the point of final sale. For example, sales taxes paid by the manufacturer are typically added to the price charged to the wholesaler or retailer and are accordingly built into the final sales price but not called a tax. Therefore, the consumer actually loses purchasing power by the amount of these taxes. In this book the purchasing power loss has been given back to the family as one of the components of total before-government income.

Total Before-Government Income: is the term used in this book to designate the amount of income the family would have received in the absence of government taxation and transfer payments. It is composed of full cash income, **less** income from government (transfer payments) **plus** hidden income and hidden purchasing power loss.

Poverty Line Income: in this Guide, the poverty line level is exactly one-half of average income in a particular year.

High Income: the high income family is one whose income is twice the average income in any given year.

"The Poor": if all families are 'lined up' from lowest to highest income, 'the poor' are the first 33 per cent of families.

"The Average": is the middle third of families.

"The Rich": if all families are 'lined up' from lowest to highest income, 'the rich' are the last 33 per cent of families.

ABOUT TAXES

Tax Burden: is the means of determining who ultimately pays tax and is synonymous with the term "tax incidence". The burden of taxes assessed by government can be shifted and in some cases is shifted **forward** to consumers, such as in the 25 per cent portion of the Corporate Profits Tax reflected in higher prices, or **backward** onto labour and capital in the form of lower wages and lower profits. Tax burden is measured by the decline in real purchasing power that results from the imposition of a tax. Shifting has been incorporated in the tax burden estimates in this Guide.

Effective Tax Rate: refers to the percentage of a family's total purchasing power that is taken away by government in the form of taxes.

Explicit Taxes: are taxes which are paid directly by the family. Examples of explicit taxes are personal income tax and provincial retail sales taxes.

Hidden Taxes: are taxes that are concealed in the price of articles that one buys. Examples of hidden taxes are the tobacco tax, manufacturers' sales taxes and import duties.

Social Security Taxes: are composed of both Federal and Provincial taxes. The Federal category includes one-half employer and employee contributions to Public Service Pensions and employer and employee contributions to Unemployment Insurance. Provincial Social Security taxes include one-half of employer and employee contributions to Public Service Pensions, employer and employee contributions to Workers' Compensation and Industrial Employees' Vacations. Also included in this category as taxes are payments to the Canada and Quebec Pension Plans and Medical and Hospital Insurance Premiums.

Corporate Profits Tax: is the tax paid on the profits of a corporation. It is assumed in this Guide that corporate profit taxes are paid 75 per cent by the shareholders and 25 per cent by the consumers which is reflected in the price paid for the final product. For a more detailed explanation, see the footnote on page 10 .

Progressive, Proportional and Regressive Taxation: these are terms which refer to the proportionality of taxes to income. A tax is called **proportional** if it takes the same fraction of income from low income people as it does from high income people. (Unemployment Insurance payments and Canada Pension payments up to the maximum earnings level are examples of proportional taxes). A **progressive tax** is one that takes a greater proportion of income from high income people than from those with low incomes (income tax, for example). A **regressive tax** is one that takes a greater proportion of income from low income people than it does from high income people (sales tax, for example).

"T1 Tax Return": is the Revenue Canada income tax form which must be completed and filed by all Canadians who receive income.

Negative Tax: See "Income from Government" in the previous section.

Taxing Powers under the Constitution of Canada: the general scheme of taxation in the British North America Act might be summarized in this way:

1. the federal government is given an unlimited power to tax;

2. the provinces are also given what amounts to an unlimited power to tax "within the province", that is to say an unlimited power to tax persons within their jurisdiction and to impose taxes in respect of property located and income earned within the province. (They may not, however, levy indirect taxes.) But their taxing powers are framed in such a way as to preclude them from imposing taxes which would have the effect of creating barriers to interprovincial trade, and generally from taxing persons and property outside the province.

PART ONE

introduction

WHAT THEY SAID ABOUT TAXES

"Alexander being asked why he did not gather money and lay it up in a public treasury, 'For fear', said he, 'lest, being keeper thereof, I should be infected and corrupted.'"
(Venning)

"Taxation on the necessaries of life is a curse equal to the barrenness of the earth and the inclemency of the weather."
(Adam Smith, the Father of Economics)

"In general, the art of government consists in taking as much money as possible from one class of citizens to give to the other."
(Voltaire in *Money*)

"In Canada, the federal government was able to meet its financial responsibilities with revenue raised by indirect taxes, such as tariffs, until 1916. During the third year of World War I, to help support a war economy, the Canadian Parliament passed the Income War Tax Act as a 'temporary measure.'"
(Revenue Canada Taxation Pamphlet 1975)

"The promises of yesterday are the taxes of today."
(Mackenzie King, Leader of the Opposition, replying to the Conservative Budget, House of Commons, June 16, 1921)

Introduction

One of the most talked about aspects of Canadian life during recent times is the extent to which the price of everything keeps rising faster and faster. Next to the weather, inflation is probably Canada's number one casual-conversation topic.

reproduced by permission of the Spectator, Hamilton

Daily exposure to rising prices on the things that we buy and monthly reminders from Statistics Canada in the form of the Consumer Price Index serve to keep inflation constantly before the public eye.

A consequence of this constant public exposure to inflation is that people not only talk about it, but also worry about it. So much so that inflation is acknowledged to be the most important problem facing Canada today. This concern about inflation naturally leads to investigations to understand its cause and find its cure.†

One result of the concern about and study of inflation is a growing realization about the extent to which governments at all levels, federal, provincial and municipal, are taking away the private citizens' ability to spend the fruits of their labours. At the present time (1976), governments at all levels spend, in total, more than 40 cents out of every dollar earned in Canada. This represents a staggering 229 per cent increase over the ten year period since 1966 and can be compared to a 66 per cent increase in the Consumer Price Index and a 150 per cent increase in total spending *(Gross National Expenditure)* during that same period.

In more graphic terms, the average Canadian now works Monday, and most of Tuesday in order to "support" government. As recently as 15 years ago the average Canadian worker was able to satisfy his "obligation" to government in just over one working day. It is interesting to note that the recent encroachment of government on private spending power is only paralleled by that achieved under the sweeping authority associated with the waging of the Second World War.

This fact about government spending is in itself worrisome. It reflects a substantial decline in the ability of Canadians to determine how they dispose of the fruits of their labours. It represents a loss of personal choice for the individual and a corresponding growth in the power of govern-

---

†The government's anti-inflation program of wage and price controls is Canada's major current attempt to deal with inflation. The Fraser Institute has recently published a book, *The Illusion of Wage and Price Control,* that critically evaluates the government's anti-inflation program. *(The Illusion of Wage and Price Control: Essays on Inflation, its Causes and its Cures ISBN 0-88975-001-7)*

ments over individuals. The transfer to government of the individual's spending power is a trend about which every Canadian should be concerned. It is a trend which concerns the Fraser Institute and that is why we have published this book.

This Fraser Institute Guide is concerned with the price that Canadians pay for government and its growth. It poses and answers the questions:

Who pays for government?

How much do they pay?

While answering these questions, the Fraser Institute developed several new measures of the cost of government to Canadians. We call one of these measures the "Canadian Consumer Tax Index". This measure will be calculated and released by the Fraser Institute at regular intervals. The intervals will be, in part, determined by how often Statistics Canada conducts its surveys of income and expenditure. We believe a Consumer Tax Index (or CTI) ought to have as much relevance and significance for Canadians as the well-publicized Consumer Price Index (or CPI).

5

PART TWO

calculating the tax payable

"Taxes are far from being a modern invention. The oldest known tax form — a clay tablet with cuneiform impressions — shows that income taxes were being levied 4,500 years ago. Then, a rich farmer paid 10% of his harvest in the form of cows, fish and grain. Many things have changed since that farmer's time, but taxes remain."
(Revenue Canada Taxation Pamphlet 1975)

Calculating the Tax Payable

Figuring out the amount of sales tax due on an item is a detail that the accomplished department store clerk takes in stride, except of course, at those irksome junctures when the tax rate is changed. Calculating the duty due on a long-awaited imported article is merely the last minor irritation in a sequence and is quickly forgotten as the parcel and the memory of the irritation are carried home. Even personal income tax calculations are still within the ken of most Canadians — though the odds of passing the 'T1 Tax Return' maze unscathed are diminishing.

"T1 time again. My happiest season."

The growing complexity of an individual's income tax calculation has been reflected in the corresponding growth of the "tax consultant" industry. Although income tax calculation is complicated and increasingly so, it is a mere shadow of the effort required to unravel the actual tax position of the average Canadian. A variety of factors is responsible for this complexity. The first is the fact that almost 40 per cent of the taxes the average Canadian pays are *hidden* taxes. They are *hidden* in the sense that they are not identified as taxes when they are collected from the consumer. Furthermore, it is not easy for the average consumer to "unravel" the layers of transactions that hide these taxes. The second reason, and a further complication, is the fact that some of the income produced by the efforts of the consumer does not show up in his regular paycheque or other familiar money payments.

For example, most Canadians (though some are unaware of it) either directly or indirectly through their pension fund, life insurance policies, registered retirement savings or homeownership plans, are owners of shares in Canadian corporations. The income or profit of these corporations belongs, ultimately, to its shareholders and therefore the taxes on corporate income have to be included in the consumer's tax total. Some of these taxes on profit are passed on directly to the consumer in the form of higher prices. It is not immediately apparent (or even apparent after some lengthy consideration) how the profits and the taxes on them should be allocated to the consumers who ultimately pay them. In this Guide we have assumed that one-quarter of the tax on corporate profits is passed on to the consumer in the form of a higher price. The other three-quarters are assumed to be paid out of the profits that would otherwise have gone to the shareholders.†

Similarly, many of the tax dollars that we pay are imbedded in the prices of the items that we buy. For example, when someone buys a yo-yo, or suchlike indispensable item,†† he pays a sales tax on the purchase price (unless he happens to buy it in Alberta which has no sales tax). But included in the purchase price are sales taxes paid by the

---

†The reader may well wonder why we have selected one-quarter of the tax as the amount passed on to the consumer — instead of two-thirds or three-quarters. The rationale behind the split is one of the many subjects upon which there has been an academic feast. We have simply followed the conventional wisdom as contained in Maslove, cited opposite. The effect of using a one-quarter pass-on is that the bulk (three-quarters) of the tax is assumed to be paid by consumers in their capacity as shareholders as outlined in the text. All consumers pay the "passed-on" portion of the profit, while only those consumers who are also shareholders pay the tax that cannot be passed on. A more detailed discussion of this can be found in Maslove, pages 39-40.

††We use "yo-yo" in preference to "widget" as an early and clear indication of the radical departures contained in this book.

manufacturer and all the other taxes on the wood, the string and the paint. Furthermore, if the raw materials for any of these components were imported, they were probably also subject to import duties when they entered Canada. Accordingly, to the extent that the final sales price reflects the taxes paid at the various earlier stages of production, the sales tax represents a tax, on a tax, on a tax.

Clearly, the problem of calculating both the hidden and explicit taxes paid by the average Canadian is not a simple matter. Indeed, it is a very complicated matter and the methods used to make the calculations are the subject of many detailed studies, including a Fraser Institute study which provided the information for this book.† In this short Guide, our objective is to summarize aspects of the more extensive study and to extract from it some commonsense measures of taxation that are meaningful to the taxpayer who has neither the time nor the inclination to get absorbed in the spongy pursuit of the details.

†Fraser Institute Technical Report 76-01, *An Analysis of Income and Taxation in Canada, 1961-1972*, S. Star and S.C. Pipes, Mimeo, 1976 (available at cost, on request, from the Institute). Some of the most important studies in this area which have influenced this book are: Allan M. Maslove, *The Pattern of Taxation in Canada*, Economic Council of Canada, December 1972; W.I. Gillespie, *The Incidence of Taxes and Public Expenditures in the Canadian Economy*, Studies of the Royal Commission on Taxation, No. 2, Queen's Printer, 1966; Joseph A. Pechman and Benjamin A. Okner, *Who Bears the Tax Burden?*, The Brookings Institution, 1974. For a complete listing of the sources used to prepare this Guide, see the bibliography.

PART THREE

how much do you pay for government?

"There is one difference between a tax collector and a taxidermist — the taxidermist leaves the hide." (Mortimer Caplan, Director of the U.S. Bureau of Internal Revenue, *Time*, Feb. 1, 1963)

How Much Do You Pay For Government?

"I'm telling you for the last time, Harwick. It's none of your business how much it costs the taxpayers. Your job is to fire that gun."

Drawing by Alan Dunn; © 1941,
1969 The New Yorker Magazine, Inc.

In a recent publication entitled *Perspective Canada*, Statistics Canada, the country's official statistical agency, produced a chart that showed how Canadians have been spending their incomes. According to this chart,† taxes in a recent year amounted to only 18 per cent of income. But they neglected to indicate that sales and all other hidden taxes were not included in their measure of taxes. In the January 1976 edition of the *Canadian Statistical Review*, 'StatCan' produced an estimate of income and income taxes for 1974 that indicated that the average rate of income tax was 14.5 per cent. Now, although these numbers are not comparable and certainly were not meant to give the impression that the overall tax

†Statistics Canada, *Perspective Canada*, Chapter 8, Chart 8.2, Disposition of Total Personal Income, p. 181.

rate is falling, they do illustrate an important aspect about Canadians and their taxes. That is, there is much information around about the tax bill the average Canadian pays that could unintentionally mislead the unwary.

Most economists - those at Statistics Canada included - are aware of the fact that most of the official published information about taxes does not allocate the hidden tax burden and therefore does not tell the full tax story. Some economists have in the past tried to measure this true tax cost but their work has not received the attention it deserves. In particular, the fruits of their efforts are not reflected in the "official" statistics purporting to show how Canadians spend or "dispose of" their income. The official reason for this omission by Statistics Canada, in spite of the fact that the information to produce such estimates exists, is that there are "unresolved methodological" issues. (That is, there is no common agreement about the methods that should be used to make the estimates). It is also argued that the construction of estimates would involve making certain assumptions that might be found "questionable". What should be made clear is the fact that current procedures at Statistics Canada of the sort mentioned above do contain an implicit estimate of hidden taxes. This estimate implies, in effect, that there are no hidden taxes, an assumption that all agree is wrong.

What we hope to do in this Guide is to make these hidden taxes explicit and to make an attempt at allocating them to the people who actually pay them. We are doing it in the spirit that such an estimate is better than zero and that some light shed on the subject is better than total darkness.

The crucial questions

In this vein, we have addressed the following sorts of questions:

How much tax does the average Canadian pay?

How has this tax payment changed through the years?

How much tax do YOU the reader pay?

How has your tax burden changed during the past 15 years?

How does the increase in your tax payments compare with the increase in your payments for food, shelter and clothing over the same period?

Using the tables at the back of this Guide it is possible for you to estimate answers to these questions based on averages for taxpayers throughout Canada. As an illustration of how the tables can be used we will, in the following sections, use the tables to calculate the taxes paid by an average Canadian family in 1961, 1969, 1972 and 1975. From the taxes paid by the average Canadian family in each of these years we have constructed our measure of the changing burden of taxes over time — the Consumer Tax Index.

For the purpose of constructing the examples we had to identify the mythical "average Canadian family" — or at least, a Canadian family that had average income. In each of the years we examined, this family, though average in each year, had different characteristics in each year. For example, in 1961 the family that earned an average income had 3.6 family members on average, while in 1972 the average income family had only 3.3 members, reflecting smaller family sizes. Similarly, the age of the head of the average household fell from 43 in 1961 to 41 in 1972. The family with average income was more likely to own a car in 1972 than it was in 1961 but less likely to own a house.

In reflecting on these facts it is important to note that the average family is truly mythical in the sense it does not correspond to any given real family. The average includes young families whose income, family size and assets are usually increasing and elderly households whose income, size and assets are usually all decreasing. To some extent, this averaging across types of families blurs the impression gained from analyzing the information. However, this imperfect focus does not affect our use of the "average" family as a device to enable us to see how the tax system has changed over a period of time.

Fortunately, we were able to use the survey information obtained by Statistics Canada and published as *The Family Expenditure Survey* to isolate the average income family. This survey, measuring the spending patterns of a wide-ranging sample of families, enables researchers to determine not only the average income family but also, more importantly, how this average family spends its income.

How the average Canadian family spends its income

Many of the taxes paid by the family are "collected" when the family spends its income. Sales taxes (both explicit and hidden), import duties, excise taxes, property taxes, etc. are all included in the price that the family pays for its food, clothing, shelter and other goods and services. So, in order to determine the family's true tax bill we have to determine how much of its income the family spends on each of a wide

range of products. The taxes paid, of course, vary from family to family as the pattern of spending on high and low tax items changes. For example, alcohol is a highly-taxed item and if a particular family spends much of its income on alcohol it will pay a high tax bill while spending its income. That is, "high" relative to a family that spends none of its income on alcohol.

Fortunately, the pattern of spending for families with similar incomes tends not to vary too much and so we are able to use the information collected by Statistics Canada to estimate the pattern of family expenditure and then estimate the pattern of taxes paid by families when they spend their income. For the purposes of this Guide, we have calculated the taxes paid at the time of purchase for each income level by applying the spending pattern that Statistics Canada says was typical for a family with that particular income.

The reader who had a fairly firm grasp of the notion "average Canadian family" before reading the foregoing will probably now have reason to agree with the view that "economists are those experts who manage to tell you something you know to be wrong, in language you can't understand, about something which is of no earthly importance". But bear with us — on average we had good reason for the detour through these marshy areas. The important stepping stones are:

1. that the "average Canadian family" for our purpose is one having income that was average in each of the years that we examine;

2. that a family with that income is assumed to have spent it in each year in a way typical for the average income group in that year;

3. that a family with average income may not have been average in other respects — number of members, age of head of household, etc.

How much tax?

In order to calculate the amount of tax Canadians pay it is necessary first to determine exactly how much income they earn. The ultimate objective is to determine what the families' incomes would have been in the absence of government taxation and transfer payments. As we indicated in an earlier section, some of the income Canadians earn is *hidden* in the sense that most of us are conscious neither of it nor of the taxes we pay on it. In order to determine how much tax a particular Canadian family pays we must also determine how much hidden income the family earns. Because of the fact that all of the information we have about income consists of averages we must be satisfied with determining average "hidden" income. (Accordingly, the hidden income calculated for a particular group may or may not exactly correspond to the reader's "hidden" income even if the reader is in that income group. But it will be the best estimate that can be made with the available information.)

In addition to hidden income we must also account for income which, though directly received in one form or another, would not be "counted" by some people since it is not received in a regular "payroll" form; for example, interest accumulated on bank deposits, savings bonds and insurance premiums. These and other forms of income are inadvertently (or purposely) neglected by some Canadian families when they are surveyed by Statistics Canada (a lapse which the tax man is unfortunately adept at pointing out †). In constructing our tables, we have taken this "underreporting" problem into account. Although ignoring it would not affect the calculation of the tax bill, it would and does affect the calculation of the effective tax rate. We suggest that when calculating their incomes readers use the same income that they would report if they were responding to a Statistics Canada spending survey.

---

† Although in the 1975-76 taxation years, interest income and/or grossed-up dividend income from Canadian corporations of up to $1,000 is tax exempt.

Peeling the income onion

Family income is the means whereby the family is able to exercise purchasing power. Taxation is the means whereby governments take away part of this purchasing power. In order to measure the full burden of this transfer of purchasing power it is necessary to determine what family purchasing power would have been in the absence of government. We have engaged in these arithmetic gymnastics so that we could determine what the total before-government income of families was in the three years for which we have information and to make an estimate for 1975. In order to calculate what his or her income would have been in the absence of government taxation in 1975, the reader need only look it up in the income tables in Part Six. [For reader convenience the 1975 table only has been repeated on the opposite page (Table 1). Detailed instructions on the use of the income tables are included in Part Six. If your family's income in 1975 exceeded $32,000 you will have to use the detailed income calculation table, also provided in Part Six.] The numbers in column one of the table are surveyed income or family cash income as we normally think of it. If your income does not happen to coincide with the income tables shown, pick the one closest to it. It is possible to get a more accurate estimate, but to pretend undue precision would perhaps be misleading. (If somebody from Statistics Canada asked you what your income was for the year, the amount that you would report is the appropriate one to use.) The table also shows you:

1. **what your total money income was** (column 2)

2. **how much money you received from government in one form or another** (column 3)

3. **how much hidden income you probably had** (column 4)

4. how much hidden tax you paid in the price of the articles you bought; we refer to this as your "hidden purchasing power loss" (column 5)

5. how much total income you would have had in the absence of government taxation and transfer payments (column 6).

TABLE 1
1975 INCOME TABLE

YOUR CASH INCOME	YOUR FULL CASH INCOME	LESS INCOME FROM GOV'T	PLUS HIDDEN INCOME	PLUS HIDDEN PURCHASING POWER LOSS	EQUALS TOTAL BEFORE-GOV'T INCOME †
		(DOLLARS PER FAMILY)			
Col. 1	Col. 2	Col. 3	Col. 4	Col. 5	Col. 6
2500	3300	1911	287	308	1983
3000	3825	1941	319	403	2606
3500	4380	1891	388	527	3403
4000	4950	1823	465	657	4250
4500	5519	1754	543	788	5097
5000	6051	1422	576	1100	6306
5500	6541	1038	584	1426	7514
6000	6972	1112	609	1364	7833
6500	7402	1187	633	1302	8151
7000	7888	1216	688	1344	8704
7500	8416	1215	762	1454	9416
8000	8943	1215	836	1564	10128
8500	9442	1183	900	1673	10830
9000	9888	1055	934	1784	11551
9500	10325	930	968	1893	12256
10000	10891	969	1023	1999	12945
10500	11466	992	1077	2110	13661
11000	12026	948	1122	2229	14431
11500	12584	907	1171	2348	15195
12000	12964	911	1225	2426	15705
12500	13352	914	1281	2506	16228
13000	13849	902	1345	2643	16935
13500	14356	888	1406	2793	17667
14000	14887	873	1471	2949	18434
14500	15418	858	1535	3107	19202
15000	15877	845	1591	3241	19864
15500	16404	840	1738	3359	20661
16000	16931	835	1885	3477	21458

(Continued)

23

TABLE 1 (Continued)
1975 INCOME TABLE

YOUR CASH INCOME	YOUR FULL CASH INCOME	LESS INCOME FROM GOV'T	PLUS HIDDEN INCOME	PLUS HIDDEN PURCHASING POWER LOSS	EQUALS TOTAL BEFORE-GOV'T INCOME †
		(DOLLARS PER FAMILY)			
Col. 1	Col. 2	Col. 3	Col. 4	Col. 5	Col. 6
16500*	17457	830	2032	3595	22254
17000	17984	825	2179	3713	23051
17500	18511	820	2326	3831	23848
18000	19038	815	2473	3949	24645
18500	19565	810	2620	4067	25442
19000	20092	805	2767	4185	26239
19500	20618	801	2914	4303	27034
20000	21145	796	3061	4421	27831
20500	21672	791	3208	4539	28628
21000	22199	786	3355	4657	29425
21500	22726	781	3502	4775	30222
22000	23253	776	3649	4893	31019
22500	23779	771	3796	5011	31815
23000	24306	766	3943	5129	32612
23500	24833	761	4090	5247	33409
24000	25360	756	4237	5364	34205
24500	25887	751	4384	5482	35002
25000	26413	746	4531	5600	35798
25500	26940	741	4678	5718	36595
26000	27467	736	4825	5836	37392
26500	27994	731	4972	5954	38189
27000	28521	726	5119	6072	38986
27500	29048	721	5266	6190	39783
28000	29574	717	5413	6308	40578
28500	30101	712	5560	6426	41375
29000	30628	707	5707	6544	42172
29500	31155	702	5854	6662	42969
30000	31682	697	6001	6780	43766
30500	32209	692	6148	6898	44563
31000	32735	687	6295	7016	45359
31500	33262	682	6442	7134	46156
32000	33789	677	6589	7252	46953

† The result from totalling across the columns may differ slightly from the total figure in this column. The discrepancy is due to rounding.

* See "How to Use the Income Tables", p. 67

Source: The 1975 Income Table was constructed by using Table 16 in this Guide and Statistics Canada data on income for 1975. For more information see Fraser Institute Technical Report 76-01.

How much income?

In 1975, for example, the average Canadian family surveyed reported cash income of about $14,000. The allowance for underreporting was calculated to be about $887, which is about 6 per cent of reported income. Average family cash income was thus $14,887. In order to calculate total taxable income we have to account for two additional sources of income. One of these is the "hidden" income mentioned in an earlier section.

Hidden income

For the most part, hidden income is made up of payments made by a person's employer to purchase some service for the employee — largely employer contributions to pension, medical, insurance and other private employee benefit programs. In 1975 the average income family received a total of $381 in this form alone. (This hidden income may appear to be rather low given the relatively substantial fringe-benefit packages that have evolved over the last twenty years. However, it must be remembered that this figure is an across-the-board average and therefore includes both self-employed people who have no fringes as such and people who have generous fringe-benefit packages.) Corporate profits, of which the average family owns a share through direct ownership of shares or through a pension or registered retirement savings plan of some sort, represented a further $123 of hidden income during 1975. The income that corporations retained during the year contributed a further $210 to the hidden income total. Hidden income also includes such imputed items as farm and non-farm rents and interest. Food and fuel grown and consumed on the farm also constitute part of hidden income but as the trend to move from rural to urban areas has increased in recent years, this item is virtually insignificant.

In total, for the family that was average, hidden income during 1975 amounted to a quite substantial $1,471 while actual cash income was $14,887. The same family probably would have reported its income as about $14,000 in the Statistics Canada Income and Expenditure Surveys for that year.

25

One last detour

Earlier we talked about the fact that some taxes are included in the prices of the things we buy. These taxes are called "indirect" taxes since they are not paid directly to the government by the person who really pays them but by an intermediary who pays the tax to government and then increases the price to offset the cost of the tax. For example, the price of gasoline is largely made up of tax paid by the gasoline company and then passed on to the consumer in the price at the pump. Also included with "indirect" taxes are taxes which, in this Guide, are assumed to be passed forward to the consumer in the form of higher prices for products. An example is the 25 per cent share of the Corporate Profits Tax. Now because these taxes are hidden in the price of the things we buy, the money we spend has less purchasing power than it would have had if there were no tax built into the price. Each dollar we spend pays for some good or service and some tax. If there were no tax, each dollar would buy more of a good or a service. Accordingly, in order to measure the purchasing power families would have had in the absence of government it is necessary, in effect, to give them back the purchasing power absorbed by hidden taxes. The adjustment required to do this for the average family in 1975 worked out to $2,949. This is a large figure and is an indication of the extent to which hidden taxes absorb the purchasing power of the average family. More will be said about this in a later section.

A significant omission from the calculation of hidden purchasing power loss is the effect that import duties have on the price of articles. If an import duty is effective it will deter the importation of certain goods and the lack of effective competition will almost certainly cause the Canadian price of the goods to be higher. This higher price constitutes a loss of purchasing power which is not included in our calculations.

"Would you mind telling me exactly what
you are up to? What is this big
mistake you made in the government's
favour in your income tax?"

27

How much purchasing power does government take away?
Having now calculated the total amount of purchasing
power families would have had in the absence of government, we are in a position to calculate how much of that
purchasing power governments actually take away in the
real world. In order to give the reader a reference point
against which to compare his or her own tax situation, we
will calculate the income position of the average Canadian
family preparatory to calculating its tax burden in the
following section.

In 1961, the average income of a Canadian family was
about $5,500; in 1969 it was $8,000 and by 1972 had risen to
$11,000. Our calculation for 1961 yields a full cash income of
$6,119, hidden income of $744, income from government of
$371, hidden purchasing power loss of $1,133, and finally, a
total before-government income of $7,625. By 1975, before-
government income had risen to $18,434; this was made up
of $1,471 hidden income, $2,949 hidden purchasing power
loss and $14,887 full cash income. Table 2 summarizes this
information for the 1961 and 1975 period.

TABLE 2
INCOME OF THE AVERAGE CANADIAN FAMILY

YEAR	YOUR CASH INCOME	FULL CASH INCOME	TOTAL BEFORE— GOVERNMENT INCOME
	$	$	$
1961	5500	6119	7625
1965*	6750	7329	9131
1969	8000	8473	10554
1972	11000	11874	14390
1975**	14000	14887	18434

* Estimates for 1965 are ratio and trend estimates. Cash Income in 1965 was estimated
assuming that the reporting error was the same as in 1961.

** Estimates for 1975 are based on separate estimates of the 1975 income and family
distributions.

Source: Data for the years 1961, 1969, 1972 and 1975 were calculated from the Income
Tables in Part Six.

Tax and the average family

The tax tables in Part Six are geared to family cash income. [The 1975 tax table is repeated on the following pages for reader convenience (Table 3). Detailed instructions on the use of the tax tables are included in Part Six. If your family's income in 1975 exceeded $32,000 you will have to use the detailed tax calculation table also provided in Part Six.] The dollar amount in each row represents each particular tax payable by a family which has a cash income of a given amount. To determine total actual taxes paid, we simply read the dollar amount from the final column in the table. There are four different tax tables — one each for 1961, 1969, 1972 and 1975. Since information for 1975 is not yet available, the table for 1975 is our estimate based, in part, on 1975 information and, in part, on the 1972 tax table. We must again emphasize that the "taxes paid" series incorporates average expenditure patterns. This means that the dollar amount of a particular tax may over-estimate or underestimate the amount of a particular tax paid by a particular family.

29

TABLE 3
1975 TAX TABLE

YOUR CASH INCOME	PROFITS TAX	INCOME TAX	SALES TAX	LIQUOR, TOBACCO, AMUSEMENT and OTHER EXCISE TAXES	AUTO, FUEL and MOTOR VEHICLE LICENCE TAXES	SOCIAL SECURITY, PENSION, MEDICAL and HOSPITAL TAXES	PROPERTY TAX	NATURAL RESOURCES TAXES	IMPORT DUTIES	OTHER TAXES	TOTAL TAXES
					(DOLLARS PER FAMILY)						
2500	90	70	272	116	79	155	293	34	83	31	1223
3000	109	88	326	138	95	187	351	41	99	37	1471
3500	119	128	341	148	109	204	353	43	101	52	1598
4000	125	219	335	156	113	209	312	42	94	63	1668
4500	145	323	376	191	112	230	330	47	102	54	1910
5000	164	425	416	225	112	251	347	51	110	45	2146
5500	166	499	452	232	126	284	378	54	119	46	2356
6000	164	566	486	233	143	320	412	56	128	49	2557
6500	165	677	514	257	167	346	421	58	134	52	2791
7000	169	809	538	295	193	364	415	61	139	54	3037
7500	184	899	575	305	196	393	432	64	146	58	3252
8000	199	994	614	314	200	422	449	67	156	62	3477
8500	213	1084	651	323	204	451	466	72	161	67	3692
9000	228	1174	688	333	208	479	483	75	167	71	3906
9500	238	1265	735	348	225	509	504	79	176	76	4155
10000	236	1345	809	381	287	542	533	83	189	86	4491
10500	239	1498	855	388	318	570	551	84	195	90	4788
11000	251	1746	858	360	306	588	551	84	192	83	5019
11500	261	1866	901	373	339	607	560	88	201	86	5282
12000	276	1994	947	384	362	632	576	93	209	89	5562
12500	296	2132	996	394	378	655	598	98	218	93	5858
13000	314	2259	1041	404	393	678	618	102	227	97	6133
13500	333	2392	1087	414	408	702	640	108	235	101	6420
14000	349	2505	1116	417	416	728	661	110	240	103	6645
14500	366	2618	1144	420	424	753	681	114	244	106	6870
15000	383	2730	1172	423	432	779	702	117	248	109	7095
15500	400	2842	1201	426	440	804	722	120	253	112	7320
16000	412	2923	1221	428	446	822	737	122	256	114	7481

(DOLLARS PER FAMILY)

16500*	464	3040	1252	436	452	839	759	130	261	125	7758
17000	517	3157	1282	444	457	855	780	137	265	137	8031
17500	569	3275	1313	452	463	872	802	145	270	148	8309
18000	622	3392	1344	460	468	888	824	153	275	160	8586
18500	674	3509	1375	468	474	905	846	160	280	171	8862
19000	726	3626	1405	476	480	921	867	168	284	183	9136
19500	779	3743	1436	484	485	938	889	176	289	194	9413
20000	831	3861	1467	492	491	954	911	183	294	206	9690
20500	883	3978	1497	500	497	971	933	191	299	217	9966
21000	936	4095	1528	508	502	988	954	199	303	229	10242
21500	988	4212	1559	516	508	1004	976	206	308	240	10517
22000	1040	4329	1590	524	513	1021	998	214	313	252	10794
22500	1093	4446	1620	532	519	1037	1020	221	318	263	11069
23000	1145	4564	1651	540	525	1054	1041	229	322	275	11346
23500	1198	4681	1682	548	530	1070	1063	237	327	286	11622
24000	1250	4798	1712	556	536	1087	1085	244	332	298	11898
24500	1302	4916	1743	564	542	1104	1107	252	337	309	12176
25000	1355	5032	1774	572	547	1120	1128	260	341	321	12450
25500	1407	5150	1805	580	553	1137	1150	267	346	332	12727
26000	1459	5267	1835	588	558	1153	1172	275	351	344	13002
26500	1512	5384	1866	596	564	1170	1194	283	356	355	13280
27000	1564	5501	1897	604	570	1186	1215	290	360	367	13554
27500	1617	5618	1927	612	575	1203	1237	298	365	378	13830
28000	1669	5735	1958	620	581	1219	1259	306	370	390	14107
28500	1721	5853	1989	628	587	1236	1281	313	375	401	14384
29000	1774	5970	2020	636	592	1253	1302	321	379	413	14660
29500	1826	6087	2050	644	598	1269	1324	329	384	424	14935
30000	1879	6204	2081	652	603	1286	1346	336	389	436	15212
30500	1931	6321	2112	660	609	1302	1368	344	394	447	15488
31000	1983	6439	2143	668	615	1319	1389	352	398	459	15765
31500	2036	6556	2173	676	620	1335	1411	359	403	470	16039
32000	2088	6673	2204	684	626	1352	1433	367	408	482	16317

* See "How to Use the Tax Tables", p. 79.

Source: The 1975 Tax Table was constructed by using Table 20 in this Guide and Statistics Canada data on taxes for 1975.
For more information see Fraser Institute Technical Report 76-01.

By using these tax tables we are able to calculate the average Canadian family's tax position. The results of this effort are reported in Table 4. These results indicate that the total tax bill of the average Canadian family increased by a staggering 163 per cent over the twelve-year period from 1961 to 1972. Table 5 shows that taxes, expressed as a per cent of total before-government family income, had increased from 25.7 per cent in 1961 to 35.8 per cent in 1972, a level which our estimate indicates was more than maintained during 1975.

TABLE 4
TAXES PAID BY THE
AVERAGE CANADIAN FAMILY

YEAR	YOUR CASH INCOME	FULL CASH INCOME	TOTAL BEFORE-GOV'T INCOME	TAXES PAID	INCREASE IN TAXES PAID OVER BASE YEAR
	$	$	$	$	%
1961	5500	6119	7625	1960	—
1965*	6750	7329	9131	2702	38
1969	8000	8473	10554	3586	83
1972	11000	11874	14390	5152	163
1975*	14000	14887	18434	6645	239

* See footnotes to Table 2.

Source: Data for the years 1961, 1969, 1972 and 1975 were calculated from the Tax Tables in Part Six.

TABLE 5
TAX RATES OF THE AVERAGE CANADIAN FAMILY EXPRESSED AS A PERCENTAGE OF INCOME

YEAR	TAXES AS A PER CENT OF FULL CASH INCOME	TAXES AS A PER CENT OF TOTAL BEFORE-GOVERNMENT INCOME
	%	%
1961	32.0	25.7
1965*	36.9	29.6
1969	42.3	34.0
1972	43.4	35.8
1975**	44.6	36.0

* The estimate for 1965 is based on a trend estimate of the tax rate.

** The estimate for 1975 is based on the ratio of total taxes in the economy to Net National Product applied to an income base estimated from past growth in incomes. The estimate for 1975 is most likely an underestimate.

Source: The rates for 1961, 1969, 1972 and 1975 are calculated from the Income and Tax Tables in Part Six.

Table 5 reports taxes as a percentage of income; in other words, it shows the overall effective tax rate to which the average Canadian has been subjected. The tax rate relative to total before-government income is theoretically the most correct rate since it relates an all-inclusive tax bill to an all-inclusive income total. However, cash income more closely conforms to the tax and income world of common experience. Accordingly, although the tax rate on cash income is certainly not theoretically as correct, it is almost as certain to have more intuitive appeal than the tax rate on total before-government income. In the following sections we have used the theoretically correct measure of income. Readers can easily perform the calculations using cash income if they find that a more useful 'benchmark'.

PART FOUR

introducing the canadian consumer tax index

"The art of taxation consists in so plucking the goose as to obtain the largest amount of feathers with the least possible amount of hissing."
(Attributed to J.B. Colbert, 1619-1683, Louis XIV's Controller-General of Finance)

Introducing the Canadian Consumer Tax Index

Having already ventured into areas where angels fear to tread, we took the next logical step and constructed an Index of the tax bill that the average Canadian family has had to pay over the period 1961-1975; we have also made an estimate for 1965 in order to provide a more realistic graphical illustration of the way in which the tax bill has changed. The Canadian Consumer Tax Index (CTI) appears in Table 6.

TABLE 6
THE CANADIAN CONSUMER TAX INDEX
1961 = 100

YEAR	INDEX*
1961	100
1965	138
1969	183
1972	263
1975	339

* The Index is constructed from the "Taxes Paid" column in Table 4. To calculate the Index, the taxes in each year are divided by the figure in the base year, in this case, 1961 and then multiplied by 100.

Source: Table 4.

In order to convert the taxes-paid-series to an Index all we need to do is divide each year's taxes by the figure for the base year, in this case 1961, and then multiply by 100. The Index we have constructed has a value of 100 in the base year and then a value in subsequent years which reflects the percentage increase over the 1961 value. For example, the value of the Index for 1975 at 339 indicates that the tax bill of the average family in 1975 was 239 per cent higher than it was in 1961.

CHART 1 — INTRODUCING THE CANADIAN CONSUMER TAX INDEX

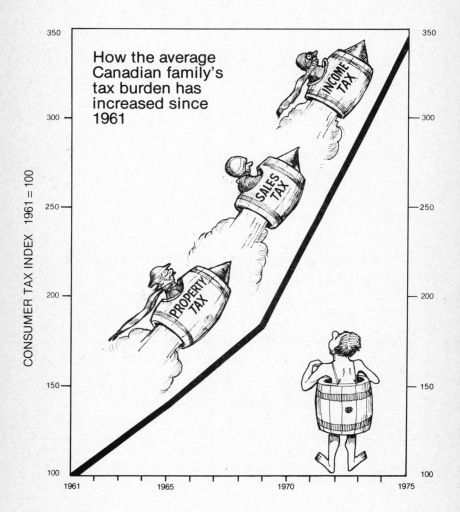

How the average Canadian family's tax burden has increased since 1961

Source: Table 6

38

The Index is an estimate — based on the best information available — of the way in which the average Canadian family's tax bill has increased over the period 1961-1975. As far as we are aware, it is the only consistent estimate that has ever been made of the way in which total tax payments for the average family have changed over the period. We offer it as the first comprehensive attempt to summarize the changing tax position of the average Canadian family. Chart 1 opposite demonstrates the rapid increase of the average Canadian family's tax burden since 1961.

What the Index shows — the tax bite compared

The Index reveals that for the average family the tax burden has increased by 239 per cent over the 1961-1975 period. To some extent, this reflects growth in income. It also reflects an increase in the overall tax rate of about forty per cent — irrespective of which of the tax rates in Table 5 one chooses to use. In order to capture the full significance of the trend reflected in the CTI it is necessary to compare the evolving tax situation of Canadians with the way in which their other expenditures are evolving.

In Tables 7, 8 and 9 on the following pages we have provided a comparison of the estimated increase in the tax burden of an average family with the increase in other claims on that family's income. At the outset, we should again stress that the Consumer Tax Index and the tax calculations imbedded in it are preliminary. Therefore, undue significance must not be attached to the precise values shown. We balance this warning, however, with the blanket warning that most economic statistics are, in fact, estimates based, in many cases, on incomplete and imperfectly measured data. So, although the CTI is preliminary and has weaknesses, it is probably as reliable as many of the statistics that Statistics Canada releases on a regular basis including the data in our Tables 7, 8 and 9.

TABLE 7
INCOME, TAXES AND SELECTED EXPENDITURES
OF THE AVERAGE CANADIAN FAMILY

YEAR	INCOME			TAXES	SELECTED EXPENDITURES †				
	AVERAGE CASH INCOME	AVERAGE FULL CASH INCOME	AVERAGE TOTAL BEFORE-GOV'T INCOME	AVERAGE TAXES PAID	AVERAGE SHELTER EXPENDITURES	AVERAGE FOOD EXPENDITURES	AVERAGE CLOTHING EXPENDITURES	AVERAGE AUTOMOBILE EXPENDITURES	AVERAGE SECURITY EXPENDITURES
	$	$	$	$	$	$	$	$	$
1961	5500	6119	7625	1960	1066	1305	491	490	264
1965*	6750	7329	9131	2702	1206	1513	603	756	324
1969	8000	8473	10554	3586	1347	1721	713	1023	383
1972	11000	11874	14390	5152	1794	1930	768	1213	479
1975*	14000	14887	18434	6645	2427	2168	807	1398	603

† All selected expenditure items **include** indirect taxes.

* Expenditure data for 1965 and 1975 are trend estimates (Lagrangian Polynomial Interpolations).

Source: Statistics Canada, Urban Family Expenditure, 1972, Catalogue No. 62-541; Family Expenditure in Canada, Volume I, All Canada, 1969, Catalogue No. 62-535 and Urban Family Expenditure, 1962, Catalogue No. 62-525.

Table 7 and Chart 2 compare the average dollar amount of family   cash   income, total before-government income (which includes the hidden income items discussed above), family expenditures on taxes and family expenditures on other items such as shelter and food.

CHART 2 — TAXES AND SELECTED EXPENDITURES OF THE AVERAGE CANADIAN FAMILY, 1961-1975

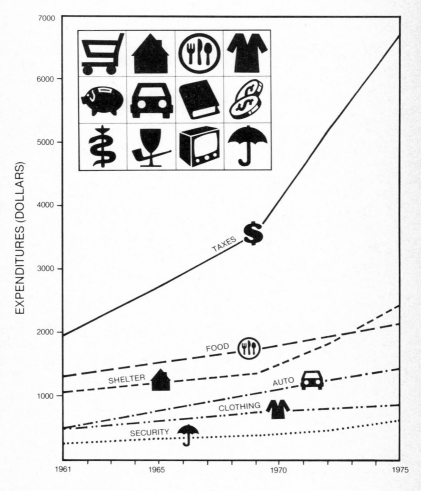

Source: Table 7

41

TABLE 8
AVERAGE CANADIAN TAX, INCOME, PRICE AND
SELECTED EXPENDITURE INDICES FOR SELECTED YEARS
1961 = 100

YEAR	TAXES CONSUMER TAX INDEX	INCOMES AVERAGE TOTAL BEFORE-GOV'T INCOME INDEX	CONSUMER PRICES CONSUMER PRICE INDEX	SELECTED EXPENDITURES † AVERAGE SHELTER EXPENDITURE INDEX	AVERAGE FOOD EXPENDITURE INDEX	AVERAGE CLOTHING EXPENDITURE INDEX	AVERAGE AUTOMOBILE EXPENDITURE INDEX	AVERAGE SECURITY EXPENDITURE INDEX
1961	100	100.0	100.0	100.0	100.0	100.0	100.0	100.0
1965*	138	119.7	107.3	113.1	115.9	122.8	154.3	122.7
1969	183	138.4	125.5	126.4	131.9	145.2	208.8	145.1
1972	263	188.7	139.7	168.3	147.9	156.4	247.6	181.4
1975*	339	241.8	184.7	227.7	166.1	164.4	285.3	228.4
Per Cent Increase 1961-75	239%	141.8%	84.7%	127.7%	66.1%	64.4%	185.3%	128.4%

† All expenditure items **include** indirect taxes.

* Expenditure data for 1965 and 1975 are trend estimates (Lagrangian Polynomial Interpolations).

Source: Table 7. The figures in Table 7 are converted to indices by dividing each series by its value in 1961 and then multiplying by 100.

Table 8 and Chart 3 provide information similar to that in Table 7 but this time in the form of indices; these indices give the reader a handy measure to compare the way taxes, prices and the consumer expenditures of the average family have risen since 1961.

CHART 3 — HOW THE CANADIAN CONSUMER TAX INDEX (CTI) HAS INCREASED, RELATIVE TO OTHER SELECTED INDICES, 1961-1975,

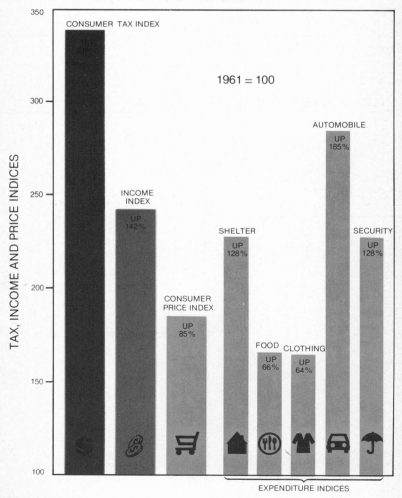

Source: Table 8

43

TABLE 9
TAXES AND SELECTED EXPENDITURES OF THE AVERAGE CANADIAN FAMILY EXPRESSED AS A PERCENTAGE OF TOTAL BEFORE-GOVERNMENT INCOME

YEAR	TAXES	SELECTED EXPENDITURES†				
		SHELTER	FOOD	CLOTHING	AUTOMOBILES	SECURITY
	%	%	%	%	%	%
1961	25.7	14.0	17.1	6.4	6.4	3.5
1965*	29.6	13.2	16.6	6.6	8.3	3.5
1969	34.0	12.8	16.3	6.8	9.7	3.6
1972	35.8	12.5	13.4	5.3	8.4	3.3
1975*	36.0	13.2	11.8	4.4	7.6	3.3

† All selected expenditure items **include** indirect taxes.

* Expenditure data for 1965 and 1975 are trend estimates (Lagrangian Polynomial Interpolations).

Source: Table 7.

Table 9 provides the same information presented earlier but expressed this time as a percentage of total before-government income, while Chart 4 opposite shows graphically how the percentage of income spent on selected items has changed during the period 1961 to 1975. The most recent estimates indicate that for the average Canadian family the 1975 tax bill represented about 36 per cent of total before-government income.

In comparing the tax bill with other expenses it should be noted that the other expenditures also include taxes. Accordingly, the comparisons in these tables and charts provide, if anything, an underestimate of the relative burden of taxation. But their message is clear. It is that taxes not only constitute the largest single claim on total family income but have also experienced the greatest increase relative to the other demands on the consumer's dollar since 1961.

CHART 4 — TAXES AND SELECTED EXPENDITURES †
OF THE AVERAGE CANADIAN FAMILY
EXPRESSED AS A PERCENTAGE OF
TOTAL BEFORE-GOVERNMENT INCOME

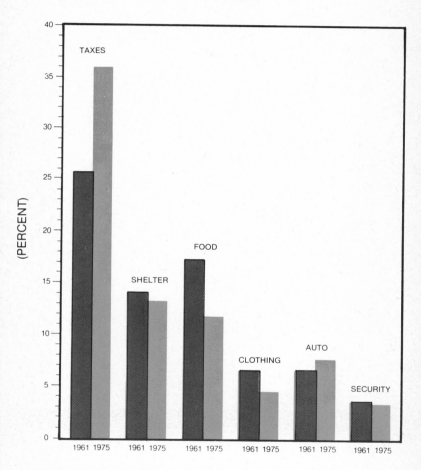

† All selected expenditure items **include** indirect taxes.

* Expenditure data for 1965 and 1975 are trend
estimates (Lagrangian Polynomial Interpolations).

Source: Table 9

45

Did you get your money's worth?

During the period 1961-1975 the average Canadian family spent a declining percentage of its income on food and clothing and devoted a slightly larger percentage to expenditures on such major items as shelter and automobiles. These expenditure patterns were associated with a fairly dramatic increase in the standard of living. Average family income has more than kept ahead of the increase in the Consumer Price Index over the past fifteen years; on the other hand, the increase in taxes has far exceeded not only price increases but the increase in family income as well. Since 1961 taxes have become an increasingly large drain on family income. From just over one-quarter of income in 1961, the tax bite has increased to the point where in 1975 it is estimated to absorb 36 per cent of the average family's income. The questions that we must ask, but which we cannot at this stage answer, are:

What did the average Canadian family receive from government in return for the 239 per cent increase in its tax bill?

Did the average Canadian family's returns from government increase by as much as the tax bill increased?

What have YOU the reader received in return for your increased tax payment?

These questions raise the whole issue of government or public expenditure but we are not really talking here about HOW your tax dollar is spent by government, important though that is. It is a simple matter to determine how much of your tax dollar is spent on various government services. The fundamental question that we are raising here is whether or not your own personal benefits *from* government have increased relative to the increased price that you are paying *for* government. Each of us should ask and answer this for ourselves.

In 1976 there is a hue and cry in Canada that there is a housing crisis for the average Canadian; there is said to be a crisis of nutrition for many; there is said to be a problem of poverty. However, while shelter expenditures for the average family have risen by 128 per cent over the past fifteen years and expenditures on food for the average family have risen by 66 per cent, tax payments have risen by 239 per cent! It is passing curious, therefore, that there is no hue and cry about the taxation crisis.

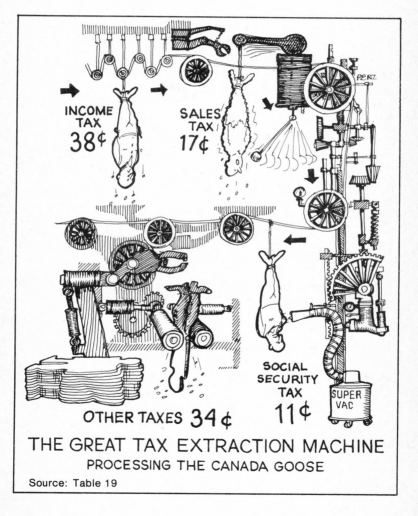

INCOME TAX 38¢

SALES TAX 17¢

OTHER TAXES 34¢

SOCIAL SECURITY TAX 11¢

SUPER VAC

THE GREAT TAX EXTRACTION MACHINE
PROCESSING THE CANADA GOOSE

Source: Table 19

The tax dollar make-up

The tax tables in Part Six also enable us to calculate an approximate breakdown of the total tax bill into its components. That is, we can calculate how much of each type of tax the average Canadian family pays. This is illustrated in Chart 5.†

About 38 per cent of total taxes in 1975 were accounted for by federal and provincial income taxes. However, in 1961, federal and provincial income taxes only accounted for approximately one-quarter of total taxes collected. It is worth noting the change in the make-up of the tax pie from 1961 to 1975. This is well illustrated in Chart 5. Not surprisingly, income taxes constitute the single biggest tax for most families and accordingly, it is the tax of which we are most aware and this fact has not changed over the fifteen year period.

Looking at the remainder of the information for 1975, we find that sales taxes account for about 17 per cent of total taxes paid but this fact is not evident since more than half of total sales taxes are hidden in the price of the article.†† At 11 per cent of the total, social security taxes (government pension plan, unemployment insurance premiums, workers' compensation, etc.) rank as the third largest government levy, followed by property taxes at about 10 per cent of total taxes; auto and fuel taxes and licence fees account for 6 per cent; liquor, tobacco and amusement taxes, also 6 per cent and corporate profit taxes, 5 per cent. Miscellaneous taxes such as import duties and natural resources taxes make up the remainder.

---

†To calculate the percentages in Chart 5, we used the 1975 Tax Table which appears in Part Six. The income of the average Canadian family in that year was $14,-000; therefore, we took each particular tax at that income level and calculated what percentage it represented of total taxes paid. The same procedure was used to establish the 1961 proportions.

††About sixty per cent of total sales taxes are Federal taxes and are paid by the manufacturer. Accordingly, they are included in the price paid for the article and not recognized as a tax.

CHART 5 — WHERE THE TAXPAYER'S TOTAL TAX DOLLAR WENT IN 1961 AND 1975

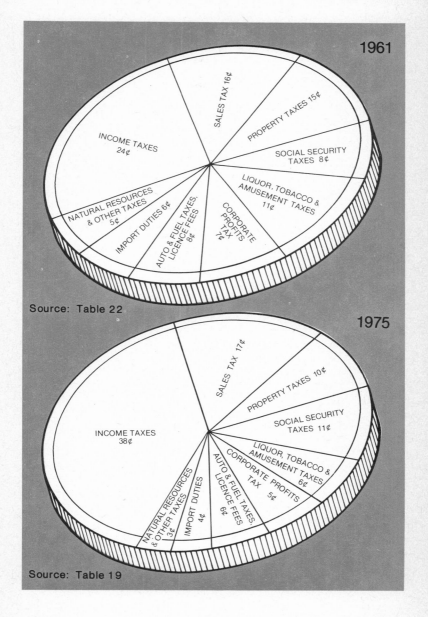

1961

SALES TAX 16¢

PROPERTY TAXES 15¢

INCOME TAXES 24¢

SOCIAL SECURITY TAXES 8¢

LIQUOR, TOBACCO & AMUSEMENT TAXES 11¢

NATURAL RESOURCES & OTHER TAXES 5¢

IMPORT DUTIES 6¢

AUTO & FUEL TAXES; LICENCE FEES 8¢

CORPORATE PROFITS TAX 7¢

Source: Table 22

1975

SALES TAX 17¢

PROPERTY TAXES 10¢

INCOME TAXES 38¢

SOCIAL SECURITY TAXES 11¢

LIQUOR, TOBACCO & AMUSEMENT TAXES 6¢

CORPORATE PROFITS TAX 5¢

NATURAL RESOURCES & OTHER TAXES 3¢

IMPORT DUTIES 4¢

AUTO & FUEL TAXES; LICENCE FEES 6¢

Source: Table 19

49

PART FIVE

the relative burden of taxation

"The taxes are indeed heavy; and if those laid on by the government were the only ones we had to pay, we might more easily discharge them; but we have many others, and much more grievous to some of us. We are taxed twice as much by our idleness, three times as much by our pride, and four times as much by our folly; and from these taxes the commissioners cannot ease or deliver us by allowing any abatement."
(Benjamin Franklin)

The Relative
Burden of Taxation

Because the tax burden of an individual family varies (even in percentage terms), according to that family's income, we have also calculated the Consumer Tax Index for both high income families and low income families. The low income family was selected as one whose income in each year was exactly half the average income. The high income family was selected as one whose income was exactly twice the average income. On a cash income basis, the low income level selected is about equal to the "poverty line" income suggested by the Senate report on poverty.†

† *Poverty in Canada, A Report of the Special Senate Committee on Poverty,* Information Canada, 1974, page 216.

The un-average Canadian

The facts yielded by these calculations are presented in Table 10. What is really striking about the information in this table is the extent to which families at all levels of income are burdened by taxation and the extent to which this burden has increased in the last 15 years. The fact that the taxman seems to be appearing more and more frequently at the door of average income and poverty line income families is also disquieting. In fact, although high income families have paid and are paying a much higher tax bill than either poverty line income or average income families, the tax *rates* for both poverty line and the average income families have increased more quickly in recent years. This result is, in part, a consequence of the fact that in calculating tax rates we have ignored the income that families receive from government. Since low income families finance many of their expenditures (in the course of which taxes are paid) with social assistance payments from government, it is somewhat misleading to ignore these payments when calculating tax rates. This is the subject of further discussion later in the Guide.

TABLE 10
INCOMES, TAXES AND TAX RATES OF HIGH INCOME, AVERAGE INCOME AND POVERTY LINE FAMILIES

INCOMES RECEIVED

	POVERTY LINE		AVERAGE INCOME		HIGH INCOME	
YEAR	YOUR CASH INCOME	TOTAL BEFORE-GOV'T INCOME	YOUR CASH INCOME	TOTAL BEFORE-GOV'T INCOME	YOUR CASH INCOME	TOTAL BEFORE-GOV'T INCOME
	$	$	$	$	$	$
1961	2750	3884	5500	7625	11000	16336
1965*	3375	4444	6750	9131	13500	19685
1969	4000	4885	8000	10554	16000	22899
1972	5500	7602	11000	14390	22000	31999
1975*	7000	8704	14000	18434	28000	40578

TAXES PAID

	POVERTY LINE	AVERAGE INCOME	HIGH INCOME
	$	$	$
1961	954	1960	5120
1965*	1320	2702	6516
1969	1748	3586	8012
1972	2340	5152	11227
1975*	3037	6645	14107

TAX RATES BASED ON TOTAL BEFORE-GOVERNMENT INCOME

	POVERTY LINE	AVERAGE INCOME	HIGH INCOME
	%	%	%
1961	24.6	25.7	31.3
1965*	29.7	29.6	33.1
1969	35.8	34.0	35.0
1972	30.8	35.8	35.1
1975*	34.9	36.0	34.8

* Data for 1965 and 1975 are trend estimates.

Source: Taxes paid for the years 1961, 1969, 1972 and 1975 are from the Tax Tables in Part Six while the incomes received are from the Income Tables, also in Part Six. Poverty Line Income equals one-half average income; High Income equals twice average income.

In 1961, the average Canadian family paid a tax bill that was nearly half as large as a high income family's tax bill. During the period of the early 60's this fraction started to fall as high income families experienced a larger increase in their tax rates than did average families. A similar relationship existed between taxes paid by poverty line families and those paid by high income families. However, by 1969 this relationship had changed, reflecting the relatively more rapid rise in the tax rates experienced by low and average income Canadian families. On the basis of the trends in the information that is available, it seems that the average Canadian family will, in the future, pay proportionately more tax than either high or low income families.

In other words, the tax system is becoming more regressive toward the average. This finding conforms to the conventional belief that the average family carries an undue share of the tax burden. At least, the evidence is that reality is gradually changing to conform to the popular view about the burden of taxation. Chart 6 opposite illustrates this point.

It might be tempting to conclude, on the basis of this information, that the tax system should be made more progressive — i.e. that there should be higher tax rates for high income families. However, as we shall see later in this section, the high income third of families already pays about 83 per cent of the total tax bill. A more promising avenue of reform would be the examination of the government taxation and expenditure process that is producing the overall tax burden — a burden that is increasingly oppressive to all Canadians.

CHART 6 — HOW MUCH TAX DO CANADIANS PAY? COMPARISON OF TAX RATES AND TOTAL TAXES PAID ON TOTAL BEFORE-GOVERNMENT INCOME

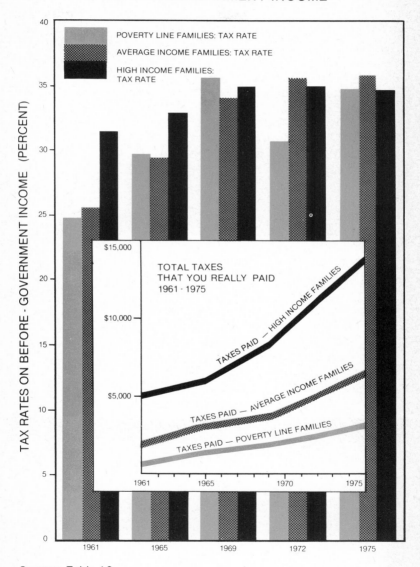

POVERTY LINE FAMILIES: TAX RATE

AVERAGE INCOME FAMILIES: TAX RATE

HIGH INCOME FAMILIES: TAX RATE

TAX RATES ON BEFORE - GOVERNMENT INCOME (PERCENT)

TOTAL TAXES THAT YOU REALLY PAID 1961 - 1975

TAXES PAID — HIGH INCOME FAMILIES

TAXES PAID — AVERAGE INCOME FAMILIES

TAXES PAID — POVERTY LINE FAMILIES

Source: Table 10

57

RAGGED DICK SERIES
BY
HORATIO ALGER JR,

TABLE 11
THE RAGS-TO-RICHES TAX BURDEN

		1961	1965	1969	1972	1975
CASH INCOME (ASSUMED)*	$	2750	5337	10357	17029	28000
TOTAL BEFORE-GOV'T INCOME	$	3884	7543	14650	23741	40578
TAXES PAID**	$	954	2187	5000	8367	14107
TAX RATE***	%	24.6	29.0	34.1	35.2	34.8

PERCENTAGE INCREASE 1961-1975

CASH INCOME (ASSUMED)	+ 918.2%
TOTAL BEFORE-GOVERNMENT INCOME	+ 944.7%
TAXES PAID	+ 1378.7%
TAX RATE	+ 41.5%

Source: *Assumed income was arrived at by assuming that income increased smoothly in equal percentage increases from poverty line level in 1961 to high income by 1975.
**Taxes are calculated for 1961, 1969, 1972 and 1975 using the Tax Tables in Part Six.
***It was assumed that the tax rate between 1961 and 1969 increased smoothly in equal percentages and that method was used to calculate the 1965 tax rate. The 1965 tax rate was applied to the total before-government income in order to get the 1965 taxes paid.

The Horatio Alger line

All of the foregoing calculations have been made on the assumption that the family concerned (whether having a high, low or average income) did not improve through time its relative position in the income distribution. A family of, say, average income was assumed to have average income throughout the period. A more realistic situation is that a family moves through a range of circumstances — starting, perhaps, at a below average income and, over time, moving to above average income and upon retirement usually returning to a more average level. The movement from below average to above average income in more dramatic terms could be described as a movement from rags-to-riches. Accordingly, in the same way that we can identify a poverty line, we can identify a "rags-to-riches" or "Horatio Alger" line. We can then calculate the tax burden associated with the move from an income level that is low (relative to the average) to an income level that is high (relative to the average).

To simplify matters we can select both the "rags" and "riches" situations from the examples that we have already constructed. Let's assume that a family on the poverty line in 1961 managed to increase its relative standing in the income distribution so that by 1975 its income was twice as high as the average (our "high" income measure). By how much would this family's annual tax burden have increased? What, approximately, was the size of the total tax impediment encountered by the family as it was trying to move from a poverty line standard of family expenditure to a "high" income standard of expenditure?

The data in Table 11 indicate that in moving from the poverty line to a "high" income during the 1961 to 1975 interval a Canadian family would have seen its tax burden increase by 1,379 per cent. In dollar terms, the annual tax bite would have increased from $954 per year to $14,107 per year — a level more than five times the total poverty line income in 1961. In the process of improving its standard of living, the family would have earned a total income of $243,535 and paid total taxes of $81,947.

Afterword

Up to this point we have analyzed the tax position of low, average and high income families. We have provided some indication of the relative burden of taxation for the average family. We have also provided the reader with the ability to calculate his or her own real tax bill. We have had little to say about the system of taxation and about what all of the details "add up" to. In other words, what would be the total result if all Canadian families were to complete the "real" tax form? The time has come to answer questions such as these. In this section, we will look at the tax system as a whole — which income group in society pays the most tax? Do high income families pay less tax than low income families?

In approaching the analysis it must be remembered that "high income" and "low income" are not clear-cut labels. For example, in 1975 the average family had income of $14,000. If a single elderly person had an income as high as this in 1975, he or she would have been quite "well-off". On the other hand, a family with four young children would have found this income sufficient, but would certainly not have considered itself "well-off". In the technical study that lies behind this Guide we have had to "average" the figures for different families and therefore our rich and poor families are mythical average rich folks and average poor folks.

To answer questions about the "rich" and the "poor" we have to identify them and that is no easy matter. For the sake of simplicity, we have divided families into three groups. We lined up all families according to their income and starting with the lowest income family we added up the taxes paid by families until we had accounted for one third of all families. This group is what we have called "the poor". The "average" group is made up of families that constituted the middle third and the remainder we call "the rich".

The results of this "adding up" (Table 12) conflict with common impressions. In the first place, the results show that the "rich" third of families pay nearly two-thirds of the total dollar tax bill while the other third is paid by poor and average families. Secondly, the results show that the situation has not changed much over the period since 1961. To some extent these results merely reflect the fact that a high proportion of the total income of Canadians is earned by those families in the top third of the income scale. In order to measure the extent to which this is true, we have constructed a table which shows how the tax "adding up" compares with the income "adding up".

TABLE 12
TAXES PAID BY LOW INCOME, AVERAGE INCOME AND HIGH INCOME FAMILIES

YEAR	LOW INCOME THIRD		AVERAGE INCOME THIRD		HIGH INCOME THIRD	
	TAXES PAID	SHARE OF TOTAL TAX	TAXES PAID	SHARE OF TOTAL TAX	TAXES PAID	SHARE OF TOTAL TAX
	$ Million	%	$ Million	%	$ Million	%
1961	988	10.7	2511	27.2	5732	62.1
1969	2753	11.4	6182	25.6	15212	63.0
1972	3335	10.2	9351	28.6	20009	61.2
1975*	4564	9.0	14149	27.9	32001	63.1

* 1975 is a Fraser Institute forecast estimate.

Source: Fraser Institute Technical Report 76-01.

Table 13 indicates that the share of the national tax burden paid by a group closely follows the share of the nation's income that the group received. However, it also shows that the lowest income group bears a disproportionately high share of the tax burden relative to the amount of income it receives. A pattern consistent with our earlier findings seems to be evolving in that the share of the tax paid by the middle income group is rising relative to the share of income that the middle income group received. The reverse pattern seems to be emerging for the highest income third of families.

TABLE 13
SHARE OF INCOME AND TAXES BY LOW INCOME, AVERAGE INCOME AND HIGH INCOME FAMILIES

YEAR	LOW INCOME THIRD SHARE OF		AVERAGE INCOME THIRD SHARE OF		HIGH INCOME THIRD SHARE OF	
	Income	Tax	Income	Tax	Income	Tax
	%	%	%	%	%	%
1961	10.3	10.7	30.5	27.2	59.2	62.1
1969	8.4	11.4	29.5	25.6	62.1	63.0
1972	7.1	10.2	28.0	28.6	64.9	61.2
1975*	6.7	9.0	27.5	27.9	65.8	63.1

* 1975 is a Fraser Institute forecast estimate.

Source: Fraser Institute Technical Report 76-01.

The overall impression yielded by these tables is that the rich pay the bulk of the taxes, but the poor pay more taxes than they "should" given their incomes. There is an important feature of this result which must be more carefully scrutinized. That is, the extent to which families receive income from government.

Although direct payments from government to families are an aspect of government spending broadly considered and as a result are outside the scope of this book, they do constitute a "negative tax" (inasmuch as they are payments *from* governments to families and taxes are payments from families *to* government). Since their inclusion in the analysis alters the overall impression given by the results we would be remiss in not making the reader aware of them.

TABLE 14
NET TAXES PAID* AND THEIR SHARE
OF THE TOTAL PAID BY LOW INCOME, AVERAGE
INCOME AND HIGH INCOME FAMILIES

YEAR	LOW INCOME THIRD		AVERAGE INCOME THIRD		HIGH INCOME THIRD	
	Net Tax Paid	Share of Total	Net Tax Paid	Share of Total	Net Tax Paid	Share of Total
	$ Million	%	$ Million	%	$ Million	%
1961	−105	−1.5	1860	27.0	5142	74.5
1969	−118	− .6	5340	27.3	14326	73.3
1972	−627	−2.5	4805	19.0	20979	83.3
	−475	−1.9	7021	27.9	18638	74.0

* Net Tax Paid is calculated by subtracting transfer payments from taxes paid.

Source: Fraser Institute Technical Report 76-01.

Table 14 contains an analysis of the tax burden inclusive of "negative taxes". It is obvious from this table that once transfer payments to families have been included a quite different impression emerges. Since low income families receive most of payments from government, the share of total taxes paid by the poorest third is a negative value indicating that this group is a net receiver of funds from government. The highest income third of the population with an average income of $20,578 was, in 1972, bearing 74.0 per cent of the total net tax burden.

The reaction of the reader to the results in this Guide may well have been, "so what! Taxes are as inevitable as death so why worry about them? Besides, my standard of living has increased substantially in spite of the taxes; so again, why worry?"

It is true that there will always be taxes; it is also true that a rising standard of general affluence obscures the impact of taxation and desensitizes the taxpayer. However, the extent of taxation is merely an indicator of a more general process of expanding government control over the day to day lives of Canadians. The rising burden of taxation reflects loss of freedom of choice in education, in health services and in old age security and it is a bellwether for loss of private choice in other areas. Further, the burden of taxation is a reflection of a general process of centralization and bureaucratization that poses a real threat to the standard of affluence about which we all have become so smug.

Thus, it is the general process which causes the trend in taxation that Canadians should be worried about. The purpose of producing this Guide and the Consumer Tax Index on a regular basis henceforth is to document the symptoms of this general process — a process about which Canadians cannot continue to say "so what".

PART SIX

your real income and tax guide

INCOME AND TAX TABLES

How to Use the Income Tables

Tables 15 to 18 are the Income Tables for 1975, 1972, 1969 and 1961 respectively. Most readers of this Guide will be able to locate within $500 their cash income for the year in question in the first column in each Income Table. The following steps will enable you to establish your full cash income, income from government, hidden income, hidden purchasing power loss and total before-government income for whichever income bracket you fall within.

Step 1. Make a rough calculation of your family's cash income from all sources for the year that you are interested in (1961, 1969, 1972 or 1975).

	$
Example: Husband's income in 1975	= 8,000
Wife's income in 1975	= 8,000
Dependent daughter's income in 1975	= 300
Total cash income	16,300

Step 2. Since the table is only calculated to the nearest $500, round off your Cash Income to the nearest $500.

Example: $16,300
Round to nearest $500   = $16,500

Step 3. If your income exceeded $32,000 for 1975; $22,500 for 1972 or 1969; or $16,000 for 1961, skip to Step 5. If not, proceed through Steps 3 and 4.

Locate the line in the 1975 Income Table that has the entry $16,500 in the first column. (The column headed "YOUR CASH INCOME").

Example: See the line with the asterisk in the 1975 Income Table.

Step 4. Read off Full Cash Income, Income from Government, Hidden Income, Hidden Purchasing Power Loss and Total Before-Government Income.

Example:

Your Cash Income	Full Cash Income	Income From Gov't	Hidden Income	Hidden Purchasing Power Loss	Total Before-Gov't Income
$	$	$	$	$	$
16,500	17,457	830	2,032	3,595	22,254

Step 5. If your cash income exceeded $32,000 in 1975; $22,500 in 1972 or 1969; or exceeded $16,000 in 1961, you will have to use the Detailed Income Calculation Schedules which follow each Income Table.

67

TABLE 15
1975 INCOME TABLE

YOUR CASH INCOME	YOUR FULL CASH INCOME	LESS INCOME FROM GOV'T	PLUS HIDDEN INCOME	PLUS HIDDEN PURCHASING POWER LOSS	EQUALS TOTAL BEFORE-GOV'T INCOME †
		(DOLLARS PER FAMILY)			
2500	3300	1911	287	308	1983
3000	3825	1941	319	403	2606
3500	4380	1891	388	527	3403
4000	4950	1823	465	657	4250
4500	5519	1754	543	788	5097
5000	6051	1422	576	1100	6306
5500	6541	1038	584	1426	7514
6000	6972	1112	609	1364	7833
6500	7402	1187	633	1302	8151
7000	7888	1216	688	1344	8704
7500	8416	1215	762	1454	9416
8000	8943	1215	836	1564	10128
8500	9442	1183	900	1673	10830
9000	9888	1055	934	1784	11551
9500	10325	930	968	1893	12256
10000	10891	969	1023	1999	12945
10500	11466	992	1077	2110	13661
11000	12026	948	1122	2229	14431
11500	12584	907	1171	2348	15195
12000	12964	911	1225	2426	15705
12500	13352	914	1281	2506	16228
13000	13849	902	1345	2643	16935
13500	14356	888	1406	2793	17667
14000	14887	873	1471	2949	18434
14500	15418	858	1535	3107	19202
15000	15877	845	1591	3241	19864
15500	16404	840	1738	3359	20661
16000	16931	835	1885	3477	21458

(Continued)

TABLE 15 (Continued)
1975 INCOME TABLE

YOUR CASH INCOME	YOUR FULL CASH INCOME	LESS INCOME FROM GOV'T	PLUS HIDDEN INCOME	PLUS HIDDEN PURCHASING POWER LOSS	EQUALS TOTAL BEFORE- GOV'T INCOME †
		(DOLLARS PER FAMILY)			
16500*	17457	830	2032	3595	22254
17000	17984	825	2179	3713	23051
17500	18511	820	2326	3831	23848
18000	19038	815	2473	3949	24645
18500	19565	810	2620	4067	25442
19000	20092	805	2767	4185	26239
19500	20618	801	2914	4303	27034
20000	21145	796	3061	4421	27831
20500	21672	791	3208	4539	28628
21000	22199	786	3355	4657	29425
21500	22726	781	3502	4775	30222
22000	23253	776	3649	4893	31019
22500	23779	771	3796	5011	31815
23000	24306	766	3943	5129	32612
23500	24833	761	4090	5247	33409
24000	25360	756	4237	5364	34205
24500	25887	751	4384	5482	35002
25000	26413	746	4531	5600	35798
25500	26940	741	4678	5718	36595
26000	27467	736	4825	5836	37392
26500	27994	731	4972	5954	38189
27000	28521	726	5119	6072	38986
27500	29048	721	5266	6190	39783
28000	29574	717	5413	6308	40578
28500	30101	712	5560	6426	41375
29000	30628	707	5707	6544	42172
29500	31155	702	5854	6662	42969
30000	31682	697	6001	6780	43766
30500	32209	692	6148	6898	44563
31000	32735	687	6295	7016	45359
31500	33262	682	6442	7134	46156
32000	33789	677	6589	7252	46953

† The result from totalling across the columns may differ slightly from the total figure in this column. The discrepancy is due to rounding.

* See "How to Use the Income Tables", p. 67.

Source: The 1975 Income Table was constructed by using Table 16 in this Guide and Statistics Canada data, on income for 1975. For more information see Fraser Institute Technical Report 76-01.

Schedule 1

1975 Detailed Income Calculation

Your Cash Income

1. Full Cash Income	= Cash Income x 1.056	=
2. Income From Government	= $677	= $ 677
3. Hidden Income	= Cash Income x .206	=
4. Hidden Purchasing Power Loss	= Cash Income x .227	=
Total Before-Government Income	= 1 – 2 + 3 + 4	=

EXAMPLE:

Your Cash Income

1. Full Cash Income	= $35,000 x 1.056	= $35,000
2. Income From Government	= $677	= $36,960
3. Hidden Income	= $35,000 x .206	= $ 677
4. Hidden Purchasing Power Loss	= $35,000 x .227	= $ 7,210
		= $ 7,945
Total Before-Government Income	= $36,960 – $677 + $7,210 + $7,945	= $51,438

TABLE 16
1972 INCOME TABLE

YOUR CASH INCOME	YOUR FULL CASH INCOME	LESS INCOME FROM GOV'T	PLUS HIDDEN INCOME	PLUS HIDDEN PURCHASING POWER LOSS	EQUALS TOTAL BEFORE-GOV'T INCOME
		(DOLLARS PER FAMILY)			
2000	2316	1484	208	190	1230
2500	3304	1924	288	306	1974
3000	3874	2065	328	392	2529
3500	4443	2206	368	477	3082
4000	4975	1928	459	641	4147
4500	5506	1649	550	806	5213
5000	6043	1346	571	1139	6407
5500	6580	1042	591	1473	7602
6000	6964	1111	608	1356	7817
6500	7348	1180	624	1240	8032
7000	7854	1135	711	1357	8787
7500	8360	1089	798	1474	9543
8000	8797	957	832	1584	10256
8500	9233	825	866	1694	10968
9000	9799	872	921	1799	11647
9500	10365	919	975	1904	12325
10000	10934	876	1022	2024	13104
10500	11503	832	1068	2145	13884
11000	11874	831	1124	2223	14390
11500	12244	830	1180	2300	14894
12000	12772	814	1245	2433	15636
12500	13300	797	1309	2567	16379
13000	13827	781	1374	2749	17169
13500	14355	764	1439	2930	17960
14000	14870	748	1615	3049	18786
14500	15385	732	1791	3168	19612
15000	15900	716	1967	3286	20437
15500	16414	699	2143	3405	21263
16000	16929	683	2319	3524	22089
16500	17444	667	2495	3643	22915
17000	17959	651	2671	3762	23741
17500	18474	635	2847	3881	24567
18000	18989	619	3022	4000	25392
18500	19503	602	3198	4119	26218
19000	20018	586	3374	4238	27044
19500	20533	570	3550	4357	27870
20000	21048	554	3726	4476	28696
20500	21563	538	3903	4594	29522
21000	22078	522	4078	4713	30347
21500	22592	502	4254	4832	31176
22000	23107	489	4430	4951	31999
22500	23622	473	4606	5070	32825

Source: The 1972 Income Table was constructed by using Statistics Canada data on income for 1972. For more information see Fraser Institute Technical Report 76-01.

Schedule 2

1972 Detailed Income Calculation

Your Cash Income

1. Full Cash Income	= Cash Income x 1.050	= _____
2. Income From Government	= $473	= $ 473
3. Hidden Income	= Cash Income x .205	= _____
4. Hidden Purchasing Power Loss	= Cash Income x .225	= _____
Total Before-Government Income	= 1 − 2 + 3 + 4	= _____

EXAMPLE:

Your Cash Income

1. Full Cash Income	= $30,000 x 1.050	= $30,000
2. Income From Government	= $473	= $31,500
3. Hidden Income	= $30,000 x .205	= $ 473
4. Hidden Purchasing Power Loss	= $30,000 x .225	= $ 6,150
		= $ 6,750
Total Before-Government Income	= $31,500 − $473 + $6,150 + $6,750	= $43,927

TABLE 17
1969 INCOME TABLE

YOUR CASH INCOME	YOUR FULL CASH INCOME	LESS INCOME FROM GOV'T	PLUS HIDDEN INCOME	PLUS HIDDEN PURCHASING POWER LOSS	EQUALS TOTAL BEFORE-GOV'T INCOME
		(DOLLARS PER FAMILY)			
2000	2239	1198	274	246	1561
2500	3053	1471	350	361	2293
3000	3566	1352	449	498	3161
3500	4078	1232	547	635	4028
4000	4573	1079	624	767	4885
4500	5068	926	700	900	5742
5000	5546	802	653	1006	6403
5500	6023	678	605	1113	7063
6000	6581	661	812	1309	8041
6500	7138	644	1018	1505	9017
7000	7561	600	946	1528	9435
7500	7983	556	874	1552	9853
8000	8473	518	936	1663	10554
8500	8963	479	998	1773	11255
9000	9547	441	1108	1911	12125
9500	10131	403	1218	2049	12995
10000	10686	360	1317	2180	13823
10500	11240	316	1416	2310	14650
11000	11635	358	1475	2387	15139
11500	12029	400	1534	2463	15626
12000	12556	404	1580	2570	16302
12500	13083	408	1626	2676	16977
13000	13609	412	1672	2783	17652
13500	14136	414	1717	2890	18329
14000	14647	417	1980	3033	19243
14500	15157	421	2243	3178	20157
15000	15668	424	2506	3322	21072
15500	16179	428	2768	3466	21985
16000	16689	431	3031	3610	22899
16500	17200	435	3294	3754	23813
17000	17711	438	3557	3898	24728
17500	18211	442	3820	4042	25631
18000	18732	445	4083	4186	26556
18500	19243	448	4345	4330	27470
19000	19753	452	4608	4474	28383
19500	20264	455	4871	4618	29298
20000	20775	459	5134	4762	30212
20500	21285	462	5397	4906	31126
21000	21796	466	5660	5050	32040
21500	22307	469	5922	5194	32954
22000	22817	473	6185	5338	33867
22500	23328	476	6448	5482	34782

Source: The 1969 Income Table was constructed by using Statistics Canada data on income for 1969. For more information see Fraser Institute Technical Report 76-01.

Schedule 3

1969 Detailed Income Calculation

Your Cash Income

1. Full Cash Income	= Cash Income x 1.037	=	_____
2. Income From Government	= $476	=	$ 476
3. Hidden Income	= Cash Income x .287	=	_____
4. Hidden Purchasing Power Loss	= Cash Income x .244	=	_____
Total Before-Government Income	= 1 – 2 + 3 + 4	=	_____

EXAMPLE:

Your Cash Income

1. Full Cash Income	= $28,000 x 1.037	=	$28,000
2. Income From Government	= $476	=	$29,036
3. Hidden Income	= $28,000 x .287	=	$ 476
4. Hidden Purchasing Power Loss	= $28,000 x .244	=	$ 8,036
Total Before-Government Income	= $29,036 – $476 + $8,036 + $6,832	=	$ 6,832
		=	$43,428

TABLE 18
1961 INCOME TABLE

YOUR CASH INCOME	YOUR FULL CASH INCOME	LESS INCOME FROM GOV'T	PLUS HIDDEN INCOME	PLUS HIDDEN PURCHASING POWER LOSS	EQUALS TOTAL BEFORE- GOV'T INCOME.
		(DOLLARS PER FAMILY)			
2000	2297	705	389	347	2328
2500	3239	741	499	524	3521
3000	3680	591	526	632	4247
3500	4121	441	552	739	4971
4000	4645	416	606	845	5680
4500	5169	390	660	950	6389
5000	5644	380	702	1041	7007
5500	6119	371	744	1133	7625
6000	6594	361	786	1224	8243
6500	7255	368	850	1327	9064
7000	7918	375	913	1430	9886
7500	8579	382	977	1532	10706
8000	9241	389	1040	1635	11527
8500	9736	385	1104	1738	12193
9000	10232	382	1305	1866	13021
9500	10728	378	1507	1994	13851
10000	11224	375	1708	2122	14678
10500	11719	371	1910	2250	15508
11000	12214	367	2111	2378	16336
11500	12709	364	2312	2506	17163
12000	13205	360	2514	2634	17993
12500	13700	356	2716	2761	18821
13000	14196	353	2917	2889	19649
13500	14691	349	3119	3017	20478
14000	15187	346	3320	3145	21306
14500	15682	342	3522	3273	26135
15000	16178	338	3723	3401	22964
15500	16674	335	3925	3529	23793
16000	17169	331	4126	3657	24621

Source: The 1961 Income Table was constructed by using Statistics Canada data on income for 1961. For more information see Fraser Institute Technical Report 76-01.

Schedule 4

1961 Detailed Income Calculation

Your Cash Income

1. Full Cash Income	= Cash Income x 1.073	=	_____
2. Income From Government	= $331	=	$ 331
3. Hidden Income	= Cash Income x .258	=	_____
4. Hidden Purchasing Power Loss	= Cash Income x .229	=	_____
Total Before-Government Income	= 1 – 2 + 3 + 4	=	_____

EXAMPLE:

Your Cash Income

1. Full Cash Income	= $18,000 x 1.073	=	$18,000
2. Income From Government	= $331	=	$19,314
3. Hidden Income	= $18,000 x .258	=	$ 331
4. Hidden Purchasing Power Loss	= $18,000 x .229	=	$ 4,644
Total Before-Government Income	= $19,314 – $331	=	$ 4,122
	+ $4,644 + $4,122	=	$27,749

76

HOW MUCH TAX
DO YOU
REALLY PAY ?

How to Use the Tax Tables

Tables 19 to 22 are the Tax Tables for 1975, 1972, 1969 and 1961 respectively. Most readers of this Guide will be able to locate within $500 their cash income for the year in question in the first column in each Tax Table. The following steps will enable you to establish how much of each type of tax (whether explicit or hidden) you paid. The final column shows your total tax bill for whichever income bracket you fall within.

Step 1. Calculate your family's cash income as you did in Step 1 and Step 2 of the Income Calculation.

Step 2. If your family's cash income exceeded $32,000 for 1975; $22,500 for 1972 or 1969; or $16,000 for 1961, skip to Step 5. If not, proceed to Step 3.

Step 3. Locate the line in the tax table for the appropriate year that has your Cash Income in the first column.

If your Cash Income was $16,500 for 1975,
locate $16,500 in the 1975 tax table.
(The line in the 1975 tax table with the asterisk). .

Step 4. Read off the tax sub-totals and total tax paid.

Your Cash Income	Profit Tax	Income Tax	Sales Tax	Liquor, tobacco, amusement & other Excise taxes	Auto, fuel & motor vehicle licence taxes
$ 16,500	$ 464	$ 3,040	$ 1,252	$ 436	$ 452

Social Security, medical & hospital taxes	Property Tax	Natural Resources Tax	Import Duties	Other Taxes	Total Taxes
$ 839	$ 759	$ 130	$ 261	$ 125	$ 7,758

Step 5. If your cash income exceeded $32,000 in 1975; $22,500 in 1972 or 1969; or exceeded $16,000 in 1961 you will have to use the Detailed Tax Calculation Schedules which follow each Tax Table.

79

TABLE 19
1975 TAX TABLE

(DOLLARS PER FAMILY)

YOUR CASH INCOME	PROFITS TAX	INCOME TAX	SALES TAX	LIQUOR, TOBACCO, AMUSEMENT and OTHER EXCISE TAXES	AUTO, FUEL and MOTOR VEHICLE LICENCE TAXES	SOCIAL SECURITY, PENSION, MEDICAL and HOSPITAL TAXES	PROPERTY TAX	NATURAL RESOURCES TAXES	IMPORT DUTIES	OTHER TAXES	TOTAL TAXES
2500	90	70	272	116	79	155	293	34	83	31	1223
3000	109	88	326	138	95	187	351	41	99	37	1471
3500	119	128	341	148	109	204	353	43	101	52	1598
4000	125	219	335	156	113	209	312	42	94	63	1668
4500	145	323	376	191	112	230	330	47	102	54	1910
5000	164	425	416	225	112	251	347	51	110	45	2146
5500	166	499	452	232	126	284	378	54	119	46	2356
6000	164	566	486	233	143	320	412	56	128	49	2557
6500	165	677	514	257	167	346	421	58	134	52	2791
7000	169	809	538	295	193	364	415	61	139	54	3037
7500	184	899	575	305	196	393	432	64	146	58	3252
8000	199	994	614	314	200	422	449	67	156	62	3477
8500	213	1084	651	323	204	451	466	72	161	67	3692
9000	228	1174	688	333	208	479	483	75	167	71	3906
9500	238	1265	735	348	225	509	504	79	176	76	4155
10000	236	1345	809	381	287	542	533	83	189	86	4491
10500	239	1498	855	388	318	570	551	84	195	90	4788
11000	251	1746	858	360	306	588	551	84	192	83	5019
11500	261	1866	901	373	339	607	560	88	201	86	5282
12000	276	1994	947	384	362	632	576	93	209	89	5562
12500	296	2132	996	394	378	655	598	98	218	93	5858
13000	314	2259	1041	404	393	678	618	102	227	97	6133
13500	333	2392	1087	414	408	702	640	108	235	101	6420
14000	349	2505	1116	417	416	728	661	110	240	103	6645
14500	366	2618	1144	420	424	753	681	114	244	106	6870
15000	383	2730	1172	423	432	779	702	117	248	109	7095
15500	400	2842	1201	426	440	804	722	120	253	112	7320
16000	412	2923	1221	428	446	822	737	122	256	114	7481

(DOLLARS PER FAMILY)

16500*	464	3040	1252	436	452	839	759	130	261	125	7758
17000	517	3157	1282	444	457	855	780	137	265	137	8031
17500	569	3275	1313	452	463	872	802	145	270	148	8309
18000	622	3392	1344	460	468	888	824	153	275	160	8586
18500	674	3509	1375	468	474	905	846	160	280	171	8862
19000	726	3626	1405	476	480	921	867	168	284	183	9136
19500	779	3743	1436	484	485	938	889	176	289	194	9413
20000	831	3861	1467	492	491	954	911	183	294	206	9690
20500	883	3978	1497	500	497	971	933	191	299	217	9966
21000	936	4095	1528	508	502	988	954	199	303	229	10242
21500	988	4212	1559	516	508	1004	976	206	308	240	10517
22000	1040	4329	1590	524	513	1021	998	214	313	252	10794
22500	1093	4446	1620	532	519	1037	1020	221	318	263	11069
23000	1145	4564	1651	540	525	1054	1041	229	322	275	11346
23500	1198	4681	1682	548	530	1070	1063	237	327	286	11622
24000	1250	4798	1712	556	536	1087	1085	244	332	298	11898
24500	1302	4916	1743	564	542	1104	1107	252	337	309	12176
25000	1355	5032	1774	572	547	1120	1128	260	341	321	12450
25500	1407	5150	1805	580	553	1137	1150	267	346	332	12727
26000	1459	5267	1835	588	558	1153	1172	275	351	344	13002
26500	1512	5384	1866	596	564	1170	1194	283	356	355	13280
27000	1564	5501	1897	604	570	1186	1215	290	360	367	13554
27500	1617	5618	1927	612	575	1203	1237	298	365	378	13830
28000	1669	5735	1958	620	581	1219	1259	306	370	390	14107
28500	1721	5853	1989	628	587	1236	1281	313	375	401	14384
29000	1774	5970	2020	636	592	1253	1302	321	379	413	14660
29500	1826	6087	2050	644	598	1269	1324	329	384	424	14935
30000	1879	6204	2081	652	603	1286	1346	336	389	436	15212
30500	1931	6321	2112	660	609	1302	1368	344	394	447	15488
31000	1983	6439	2143	668	615	1319	1389	352	398	459	15765
31500	2036	6556	2173	676	620	1335	1411	359	403	470	16039
32000	2088	6673	2204	684	626	1352	1433	367	408	482	16317

* See "How to Use the Tax Tables", p.79.

Source: The 1975 Tax Table was constructed by using Table 20 in this Guide and Statistics Canada data on taxes for 1975.
For more information see Fraser Institute Technical Report 76-01.

Schedule 5

1975 Detailed Tax Calculation

1. Profit tax	= Your Cash Income x .065	= _____
2. Income tax	= Your Cash Income x .209	= _____
3. Sales tax	= Your Cash Income x .069	= _____
4. Liquor, tobacco, amusement & other Excise taxes	= Your Cash Income x .021	= _____
5. Auto, fuel & motor vehicle license fees	= Your Cash Income x .020	= _____
6. Social security, pension, medical & hospital taxes	= Your Cash Income x .042	= _____
7. Property tax	= Your Cash Income x .045	= _____
8. Natural Resources taxes	= Your Cash Income x .011	= _____
9. Import duties	= Your Cash Income x .013	= _____
10. Other taxes	= Your Cash Income x .015	= _____

Total taxes   1 + 2 + 3 + 4 + 5 + 6 + 7 + 8 + 9 + 10   = _____

TABLE 20
1972 TAX TABLE

(DOLLARS PER FAMILY)

YOUR CASH INCOME	PROFITS TAX	INCOME TAX	SALES TAX	LIQUOR, TOBACCO, AMUSEMENT and OTHER EXCISE TAXES	AUTO: FUEL and MOTOR VEHICLE LICENCE TAXES	SOCIAL SECURITY, PENSION, MEDICAL and HOSPITAL TAXES	PROPERTY TAX	NATURAL RESOURCES TAXES	IMPORT DUTIES	OTHER TAXES	TOTAL TAXES
2000	70	50	218	92	60	121	233	27	67	25	963
2500	91	75	271	115	80	157	292	34	82	31	1228
3000	199	117	283	123	93	172	288	36	83	47	1441
3500	108	158	294	131	105	186	283	37	84	63	1449
4000	128	275	334	168	102	205	296	42	92	51	1693
4500	148	392	374	204	99	224	309	46	99	38	1933
5000	146	460	409	205	116	261	343	48	108	42	2138
5500	144	528	443	206	133	297	377	50	117	45	2340
6000	151	638	472	241	157	317	382	53	123	48	2582
6500	157	747	500	276	180	337	387	56	129	50	2819
7000	174	872	537	274	175	369	392	59	134	55	3041
7500	191	996	574	272	169	401	397	62	138	59	3259
8000	192	1074	640	302	220	433	426	66	151	68	3572
8500	192	1151	706	332	271	464	454	70	163	76	3879
9000	205	1324	723	322	264	487	468	72	165	74	4104
9500	218	1496	740	312	257	510	481	73	166	72	4325
10000	228	1607	783	326	287	531	493	77	175	75	4582
10500	238	1718	825	339	317	552	505	81	183	78	4836
11000	261	1876	876	346	333	575	525	86	192	82	5152
11500	283	2037	927	353	348	598	545	91	201	85	5468

YOUR CASH INCOME	PROFITS TAX	INCOME TAX	SALES TAX	LIQUOR, TOBACCO, AMUSEMENT and OTHER EXCISE TAXES	AUTO, FUEL and MOTOR VEHICLE LICENCE TAXES	SOCIAL SECURITY, PENSION, MEDICAL and HOSPITAL TAXES	PROPERTY TAX	NATURAL RESOURCES TAXES	IMPORT DUTIES	OTHER TAXES	TOTAL TAXES
					(DOLLARS PER FAMILY)						
12000	300	2150	955	356	356	623	566	94	205	88	5693
12500	317	2262	983	357	364	649	586	98	210	91	5917
13000	333	2375	1011	361	371	674	607	101	214	94	6141
13500	350	2487	1039	364	379	699	627	104	218	97	6364
14000	412	2610	1068	371	383	713	648	113	222	111	6651
14500	475	2734	1096	377	386	727	670	121	226	124	6936
15000	537	2857	1125	384	390	742	691	130	230	138	7224
15500	600	2981	1154	390	393	756	712	138	234	151	7509
16000	662	3104	1182	397	397	770	734	147	237	165	7795
16500	724	3227	1211	403	400	784	755	156	241	178	8079
17000	787	3351	1240	410	404	798	776	164	245	192	8367
17500	849	3474	1268	416	407	812	798	173	249	205	8651
18000	912	3598	1297	423	411	827	819	182	253	219	8941
18500	974	3721	1326	430	414	840	840	190	257	232	9224
19000	1036	3844	1354	436	418	855	862	199	261	246	9511
19500	1099	3968	1383	443	421	869	883	207	265	259	9797
20000	1161	4091	1412	449	425	883	904	216	269	273	10083
20500	1223	4214	1440	456	428	897	926	225	272	286	10367
21000	1286	4338	1469	462	432	912	947	233	276	300	10655
21500	1348	4461	1498	469	435	926	968	242	280	313	10940
22000	1411	4585	1526	475	439	940	990	250	284	327	11227
22500	1473	4708	1555	482	442	954	1011	259	288	340	11512

Source: The 1972 Tax Table was constructed by using Statistics Canada data on taxes for 1972.
For more information see Fraser Institute Technical Report 76-01.

Schedule 6

1972 Detailed Tax Calculation

1. Profit tax	= Your Cash Income x .065	=	_____
2. Income tax	= Your Cash Income x .209	=	_____
3. Sales tax	= Your Cash Income x .069	=	_____
4. Liquor, tobacco, amusement & other Excise taxes	= Your Cash Income x .021	=	_____
5. Auto, fuel & motor vehicle license fees	= Your Cash Income x .020	=	_____
6. Social security, pension, medical & hospital taxes	= Your Cash Income x .042	=	_____
7. Property tax	= Your Cash Income x .045	=	_____
8. Natural Resources taxes	= Your Cash Income x .011	=	_____
9. Import duties	= Your Cash Income x .013	=	_____
10. Other taxes	= Your Cash Income x .015	=	_____

Total taxes 1 + 2 + 3 + 4 + 5 + 6 + 7 + 8 + 9 + 10 = _____

TABLE 21
1969 TAX TABLE

(DOLLARS PER FAMILY)

YOUR CASH INCOME	PROFITS TAX	INCOME TAX	SALES TAX	LIQUOR, TOBACCO, AMUSEMENT and OTHER EXCISE TAXES	AUTO, FUEL and MOTOR VEHICLE LICENCE TAXES	SOCIAL SECURITY, PENSION, MEDICAL and HOSPITAL TAXES	PROPERTY TAX	NATURAL RESOURCES TAXES	IMPORT DUTIES	OTHER TAXES	TOTAL TAXES
2000	81	48	175	82	51	118	203	26	50	26	860
2500	96	78	210	99	70	150	239	30	59	27	1058
3000	127	137	248	123	84	177	244	36	67	30	1273
3500	158	195	285	147	98	204	249	42	75	33	1486
4000	178	272	326	163	126	231	284	47	83	38	1748
4500	198	348	366	179	154	257	319	52	91	42	2006
5000	162	447	403	203	169	290	321	50	97	45	2187
5500	126	545	440	226	184	323	322	48	103	48	2365
6000	206	643	482	352	207	352	346	59	111	54	2812
6500	286	741	524	478	229	380	370	70	118	59	3255
7000	244	843	559	370	234	406	386	68	125	61	3296
7500	201	944	593	262	239	431	401	65	131	63	3330
8000	211	1047	634	278	258	456	428	69	138	67	3586
8500	220	1150	674	293	276	480	454	72	145	71	3835
9000	249	1272	705	305	279	503	475	77	149	74	4088
9500	278	1393	736	317	281	525	496	81	153	77	4337
10000	320	1525	783	324	296	549	520	113	161	80	4671
10500	362	1657	829	330	310	573	543	145	169	82	5000
11000	375	1730	864	355	313	599	551	124	175	87	5173
11500	388	1803	899	380	315	625	559	102	181	92	5344

YOUR CASH INCOME	PROFITS TAX	INCOME TAX	SALES TAX	LIQUOR, TOBACCO, AMUSEMENT and OTHER EXCISE TAXES	AUTO, FUEL and MOTOR VEHICLE LICENCE TAXES	SOCIAL SECURITY, PENSION, MEDICAL and HOSPITAL TAXES	PROPERTY TAX	NATURAL RESOURCES TAXES	IMPORT DUTIES	OTHER TAXES	TOTAL TAXES
						(DOLLARS PER FAMILY)					
12000	391	1936	927	383	323	644	573	103	184	93	5557
12500	394	2070	956	386	332	663	587	105	187	95	5775
13000	396	2203	984	388	340	682	601	106	190	97	5987
13500	399	2336	1012	391	348	701	615	107	193	98	6200
14000	516	2459	1041	396	350	713	645	121	196	125	6562
14500	632	2581	1069	401	353	725	675	135	200	153	6924
15000	749	2704	1098	407	355	738	705	148	203	180	7287
15500	865	2827	1126	412	358	750	735	162	207	208	7650
16000	982	2950	1155	417	360	762	765	176	210	235	8012
16500	1099	3072	1183	422	362	774	795	190	214	262	8373
17000	1215	3195	1212	428	365	786	825	203	217	290	8736
17500	1332	3318	1240	433	367	798	855	217	221	317	9098
18000	1449	3441	1269	438	370	811	885	231	224	345	9463
18500	1565	3563	1298	443	372	823	915	245	227	372	9823
19000	1682	3686	1326	448	374	835	945	259	231	399	10185
19500	1798	3809	1355	454	377	847	975	272	234	427	10548
20000	1915	3931	1383	459	379	859	1005	286	238	454	10909
20500	2032	4054	1412	464	381	871	1035	300	241	481	11271
21000	2148	4177	1440	469	384	884	1065	314	245	509	11635
21500	2265	4300	1469	475	386	896	1095	327	248	536	11997
22000	2381	4422	1497	480	389	908	1125	341	252	564	12359
22500	2498	4545	1526	485	391	920	1155	355	255	591	12721

Source: The 1969 Tax Table was constructed by using Statistics Canada data on taxes for 1969. For more information see Fraser Institute Technical Report 76-01.

Schedule 7

1969 Detailed Tax Calculation

1. Profit tax	= Your Cash Income x .111	= _____
2. Income tax	= Your Cash Income x .202	= _____
3. Sales tax	= Your Cash Income x .068	= _____
4. Liquor, tobacco, amusement & other Excise taxes	= Your Cash Income x .022	= _____
5. Auto, fuel & motor vehicle license fees	= Your Cash Income x .017	= _____
6. Social security, pension, medical & hospital taxes	= Your Cash Income x .041	= _____
7. Property tax	= Your Cash Income x .051	= _____
8. Natural Resources taxes	= Your Cash Income x .016	= _____
9. Import duties	= Your Cash Income x .011	= _____
10. Other taxes	= Your Cash Income x .026	= _____

Total taxes   1 + 2 + 3 + 4 + 5 + 6 + 7 + 8 + 9 + 10   = _____

TABLE 22
1961 TAX TABLE

YOUR CASH INCOME	PROFITS TAX	INCOME TAX	SALES TAX	LIQUOR, TOBACCO, AMUSEMENT and OTHER EXCISE TAXES	AUTO, FUEL and MOTOR VEHICLE LICENCE TAXES	SOCIAL SECURITY, PENSION, MEDICAL and HOSPITAL TAXES	PROPERTY TAX	NATURAL RESOURCES TAXES	IMPORT DUTIES	OTHER TAXES	TOTAL TAXES
					(DOLLARS PER FAMILY)						
2000	90	36	126	80	35	64	137	22	53	18	661
2500	118	60	160	108	50	83	171	28	66	23	867
3000	117	107	192	131	69	99	190	29	78	28	1040
3500	117	153	223	154	87	114	209	30	90	32	1209
4000	117	213	242	168	105	126	232	30	96	35	1364
4500	117	273	261	182	122	138	255	31	102	37	1518
5000	128	369	292	201	142	151	270	34	113	41	1741
5500	138	465	322	219	162	163	285	37	124	45	1960
6000	149	561	352	238	182	176	302	40	136	49	2185
6500	175	638	382	254	195	188	322	46	146	53	2399
7000	201	715	412	271	207	200	342	52	156	57	2613
7500	227	791	442	287	220	212	362	58	166	61	2826
8000	253	868	472	304	232	224	382	63	178	65	3041
8500	279	945	502	320	245	236	405	69	189	68	3258
9000	417	1044	516	328	253	241	435	94	194	109	3631
9500	554	1143	529	336	261	246	465	119	199	150	4002
10000	692	1242	543	344	269	251	495	144	204	191	4375
10500	830	1341	557	353	277	256	525	169	209	232	4749
11000	967	1440	570	361	285	261	555	194	214	273	5120
11500	1105	1539	584	369	293	266	586	219	219	314	5494

(DOLLARS PER FAMILY)

YOUR CASH INCOME	PROFITS TAX	INCOME TAX	SALES TAX	LIQUOR, TOBACCO, AMUSEMENT and OTHER EXCISE TAXES	AUTO, FUEL and MOTOR VEHICLE LICENCE TAXES	SOCIAL SECURITY, PENSION, MEDICAL and HOSPITAL TAXES	PROPERTY TAX	NATURAL RESOURCES TAXES	IMPORT DUTIES	OTHER TAXES	TOTAL TAXES
12000	1243	1638	598	377	301	271	617	244	224	355	5868
12500	1380	1737	611	385	309	276	648	269	229	396	6240
13000	1518	1836	625	393	317	281	679	294	234	437	6614
13500	1656	1935	639	401	325	286	710	319	239	478	6988
14000	1793	2034	652	409	333	291	741	344	244	519	7360
14500	1931	2133	666	418	341	296	772	369	249	560	7735
15000	2069	2232	680	426	349	301	803	394	254	601	8109
15500	2206	2331	693	434	357	306	834	419	259	642	8481
16000	2344	2430	707	442	365	306	867	443	261	680	8845

Source: The 1961 Tax Table was constructed by using Statistics Canada data on taxes for 1961. For more information see Fraser Institute Technical Report 76-01.

Schedule 8

1961 Detailed Tax Calculation

1. Profit tax = Your Cash Income x .147 = _____
2. Income tax = Your Cash Income x .152 = _____
3. Sales tax = Your Cash Income x .044 = _____
4. Liquor, tobacco, amusement
   & other Excise taxes = Your Cash Income x .028 = _____
5. Auto, fuel & motor
   vehicle license fees = Your Cash Income x .023 = _____
6. Social security, pension,
   medical & hospital taxes = Your Cash Income x .019 = _____
7. Property tax = Your Cash Income x .054 = _____
8. Natural Resources taxes = Your Cash Income x .028 = _____
9. Import duties = Your Cash Income x .016 = _____
10. Other taxes = Your Cash Income x .042 = _____

Total taxes 1 + 2 + 3 + 4 + 5 + 6 + 7 + 8 + 9 + 10

How to Calculate
Your REAL Tax Rate

Now that you know what your Total Before-Government Income is in dollars and your Total Taxes Paid in dollars, you are in a position of being able to **actually** calculate your real tax rate. This can be done by following the five easy steps outlined below. By calculating your real tax rate you can now find what percentage of your income was paid to government in the form of taxes, ie. **YOUR REAL TAX RATE.**

Step 1. Calculate Family Cash Income.

Step 2. Calculate or look up Total Before-Government Income.

Step 3. Calculate or look up Total Taxes Paid.

Step 4. Divide Total Taxes paid by Total Before-Government Income. This is your Real Tax Rate.

Step 5. To relate your Total Tax paid to your Cash Income, divide Total Tax paid by your Cash Income.

Bibliography

1) Selected Sources

Bird, Richard M., *Growth of Government Spending in Canada*, Canadian Tax Foundation, July 1970.

Canadian Tax Foundation, *The National Finances - An Analysis of the Revenues and Expenditures of the Government of Canada, 1975-76*, Canadian Tax Foundation, 1976.

Canadian Tax Foundation, *The National Finances - An Analysis of the Revenues and Expenditures of the Government of Canada, 1974-75*, Canadian Tax Foundation, 1975.

Canadian Tax Foundation, *Provincial and Municipal Finances 1975*, Canadian Tax Foundation, 1975.

Dodge, David A., "Impact of Tax, Transfer and Expenditure Policies of Government on the Distribution of Personal Incomes in Canada", *The Review of Income and Wealth*, Series 21, No. 1, March 1975, pp. 1-52.

Gillespie, W. Irwin, *Incidence of Taxes and Public Expenditures in the Canadian Economy*, (Studies of the Royal Commission on Taxation, Number 2), 1966.

Goffman, Irving J., *The Burden of Canadian Taxation*, (Tax Paper No. 29), Canadian Tax Foundation, July 1972.

Maslove, Allan M., *The Pattern of Taxation in Canada*, Economic Council of Canada, December 1972.

Meerman, Jacob P., "The Definition of Income in Studies of Budget Incidence and Income Distribution", *Review of Income and Wealth*, Series 20, No. 4, December 1974, pp. 515-22.

Musgrave, Richard A., and Peggy B. Musgrave, *Public Finance in Theory and Practice*, McGraw-Hill, Inc., 1973.

Pechman, Joseph A., and Benjamin A. Okner, *Who Bears the Tax Burden?* (Studies of Government Finance), The Brookings Institution, 1974.

Walker, Michael, ed., David Laidler, Michael Parkin, Jackson Grayson, et al., *The Illusion of Wage and Price Control*, The Fraser Institute, 1976

2) Government Sources

Bank of Canada Review, April 1976.

Revenue Canada, Taxation, *Taxation Statistics, 1974 Edition, Analyzing the Returns of Individuals for the 1972 Taxation Year and Miscellaneous Statistics.*

_____, *Taxation Statistics, 1973 Edition, Analyzing the Returns of Individuals for the 1971 Taxation Year and Miscellaneous Statistics.*

_____, *Taxation Statistics, 1971 Edition, Analyzing the Returns of Individuals for the 1969 Taxation Year and Miscellaneous Statistics.*

_____, *Taxation Statistics, 1970 Edition, Analyzing the Returns of Individuals for the 1968 Taxation Year and Miscellaneous Statistics.*

———, *Taxation Statistics, 1963 Edition, Analyzing the Returns of Individuals for the 1961 Taxation Year.**

———, *Taxation Statistics, 1962 Edition, Analyzing the Returns of Individuals for the 1960 Taxation Year.**

Statistics Canada, *Canada Year Book*, 1974, Information Canada, Ottawa.

———, *Perspective Canada - A Compendium of Social Statistics*, Information Canada, Ottawa.

———, *Canadian Statistical Review*, Catalogue No. 11-003 E, Monthly, Information Canada, Ottawa.

———, *System of National Accounts, National Income and Expenditure Accounts, Fourth Quarter and Preliminary Annual, 1974,* Catalogue No. 13-001, Information Canada, Ottawa.

———, *System of National Accounts, National Income and Expenditure Accounts, Fourth Quarter and Preliminary Annual, 1972,* Catalogue No. 13-001, Information Canada, Ottawa.

———, *System of National Accounts, National Income and Expenditure Accounts, Fourth Quarter and Preliminary Annual, 1971,* Catalogue No. 13-001, Information Canada, Ottawa.

———, *National Accounts, Income and Expenditure, 1962*, Catalogue No. 13-201, Information Canada, Ottawa.**

———, *Income Distributions by Size in Canada, 1972*, Catalogue No. 13-207, Information Canada, Ottawa.

———, *Distribution of Non-Farm Incomes in Canada by Size, 1961*, Catalogue No. 13-521, Information Canada, Ottawa.**

———, *Income Distributions by Size in Canada, 1969*, Catalogue No. 13-544, Information Canada, Ottawa.

———, *Prices and Price Indices*, Catalogue No. 62-002, Monthly, Information Canada, Ottawa.

———, *Urban Family Expenditure, 1962*, Catalogue No. 62-525, Information Canada, Ottawa.**

———, *Family Expenditure in Canada, Volume I, All Canada, 1969*, Catalogue No. 62-535, Information Canada, Ottawa.

———, *Family Expenditure in Canada, Volume III, Major Urban Centres, 1969*, Catalogue No. 62-537, Information Canada, Ottawa.

———, *Urban Family Expenditure,1972*, Catalogue No. 62-541, Occasional, Information Canada, Ottawa.

———, *The Canadian Balance of International Payments, System of National Accounts, Fourth Quarter, 1974*, Catalogue No. 67-001, Information Canada, Ottawa.

———, *The Canadian Balance of International Payments, System of National Accounts, 1971*, Catalogue No. 67-201, Information Canada, Ottawa.

———, *The Canadian Balance of International Payments and International Investment Position, 1963*, Catalogue No. 67-201, Information Canada, Ottawa.**

———, *Local Government Finance, Revenue and Expenditure, Preliminary Estimates, 1972*, Catalogue No. 68-203, Information Canada, Ottawa.

———, *Local Government Finance, Revenue and Expenditure, Preliminary Estimates, 1971*, Catalogue No. 68-203, Information Canada, Ottawa.

———, *Local Government Finance, Revenue and Expenditure, Preliminary Estimates, 1969*, Catalogue No. 68-203, Information Canada, Ottawa.

———, *Local Government Finance, Revenue and Expenditure, Preliminary Estimates, 1968*, Catalogue No. 68-203, Information Canada, Ottawa.

———, *Local Government Finance, Revenue and Expenditure, Preliminary Estimates, 1961*, Catalogue No. 68-203, Information Canada, Ottawa.**

———, *Local Government Finance, Revenue and Expenditure, Preliminary Estimates, 1960*, Catalogue No. 68-203, Information Canada, Ottawa.**

———, *Provincial Government Finance, Revenue and Expenditure, 1972*, Catalogue No. 68-207, Information Canada, Ottawa.

———, *Provincial Government Finance, Revenue and Expenditure, 1971*, Catalogue No. 68-207, Information Canada, Ottawa.

———, *Provincial Government Finance, Revenue and Expenditure, 1969*, Catalogue No. 68-207, Information Canada, Ottawa.

———, *Provincial Government Finance, Revenue and Expenditure, 1968*, Catalogue No. 68-207, Information Canada, Ottawa.

———, *Provincial Government Finance, Revenue and Expenditure, 1961*, Catalogue No. 68-207, Information Canada, Ottawa.**

———, *Provincial Government Finance, Revenue and Expenditure, 1960*, Catalogue No. 68-207, Information Canada, Ottawa.**

———, *Federal Government Finance, Revenue and Expenditure, Assets and Liabilities, 1972*, Catalogue No. 68-211, Information Canada, Ottawa.

———, *Federal Government Finance, Revenue and Expenditure, Assets and Liabilities, 1971*, Catalogue No. 68-211, Information Canada, Ottawa.

———, *Federal Government Finance, Revenue and Expenditure, Assets and Liabilities, 1969*, Catalogue No. 68-211, Information Canada, Ottawa.

———, *Federal Government Finance, Revenue and Expenditure, Assets and Liabilities, 1968*, Catalogue No. 68-211, Information Canada, Ottawa.

———, *Financial Statistics of the Government of Canada, 1961*, Catalogue No. 68-211, Information Canada, Ottawa.**

———, *Financial Statistics of the Government of Canada, 1960*, Catalogue No. 68-211, Information Canada, Ottawa.**

* "Taxation Statistics" was published by the Department of National Revenue, Taxation Division, now Revenue Canada.

** This publication was published by the Dominion Bureau of Statistics, the former name of Statistics Canada.